VISUAL COMMUNICATING

Ralph E. Wileman
University of North Carolina

Educational Technology Publications
Englewood Cliffs, New Jersey 07632

Library of Congress Cataloging-in-Publication Data

Wileman, Ralph E.
    Visual communicating / Ralph E. Wileman.
       p.   cm.
    Includes bibliographical references (p.   ) and index.
    ISBN 0-87778-248-2
    1. Teaching—Audio-visual aids.   2. Visual communication—
Problems, exercises, etc. I. Title.
LB1043.5.W498 1993   92-23771
371.3'35—dc20   CIP

Printed in the United States of America.

Library of Congress Catalog Card Number: 92-23771.

International Standard Book Number: 0-87778-248-2.

First Printing: January, 1993.

Dedication

This book is dedicated to my teachers, Professor Lillian Frank, Otterbein College, and Professor Paul W. F. Witt, Teachers College, Columbia University.

Preface

Visual communication permeates every aspect of our lives. Modern technology gives every indication that it will expand rather than diminish. The potential for visual communication to enhance our lives and facilitate understanding is self-evident. We are embarking on a renaissance in visual communication. It is already shaking the very foundations of the communications/information enterprise. Visual communicators will be in great demand. An interesting time will be had by all, especially if you can think visually.

As a teacher I have encountered many hundreds of students. They have all exhibited growth in their ability to think visually. Their energy is boundless, their commitment is absolute, and their interest is intense. They will lead us in the visual communications renaissance.

Every former student made a contribution to this book. Given the challenge to communicate visually, they did, often with refreshing conceptualizations that contributed to my understanding of the rich potential of visuals to help people understand concepts.

This book is an all-new version of my 1980 book EXERCISES IN VISUAL THINKING. Some folks at IBM asked me to update and add to this earlier work. I did and they were given Internal Use Only rights to this version. Many people at IBM were helpful. I would like to single out Judith Vadas for her support and encouragement. Also the entire crew at Agora Publishing in Belrika Massachusetts were super to work with on the IBM version. I've expanded and edited that IBM version for your perusal here. Many people helped with this book. Deborah Hallam did most of the illustrations. She had help from John Konnecker and Trena Griffith. Tom Cox took the photographs. Mark McAllister typed up the text. Tracey Koenig prepared the Annotated Bibliography. Mary Leight and Steven Burke helped me organize my thoughts regarding the Visual Design Considerations. My old friend Dennis Wheeler gave the book its layout and cover. Thank you, Dennis, and everyone else mentioned here and also those I didn't mention because I forgot to.

My publisher, Educational Technology Publications, Inc., was very helpful in organizing and editing. Michael Forman and Jamie Kasman spent untold hours giving shape and form to every page.

I hope you find the ideas in this book meaningful and helpful as you sharpen your visual communications skills.

Ralph E. Wileman
Peabody Hall
University of North Carolina
Chapel Hill, North Carolina

Purpose and Objectives

This guide assists you in designing visuals for use in your courses, presentations, or self-instructional materials.

The purpose of this guide is to support you throughout the entire visual development process: from the identification of a need for a visual, the creation of alternative approaches to the visual, the testing of ideas and rough sketches, to the final rendering of those sketches for use in the course or presentation. The objectives are to:

- Serve as the primary resource and reference tool for visual design and development
- Provide a basic rationale for the selection of kinds and degrees of visualization
- Provide assistance in conceptualizing approaches to the presentation of numerical data, facts, processes, concepts and the like.
- Detail the basic steps in designing and developing visuals elements within the course development process
- Enhance the quality and instructional impact of visuals.

Audience

This guide is useful to anyone who wants to improve his or her use of visuals in learning environments.

Organization

The book is organized into five chapters and an appendix as follows:

- Chapter 1 (Introduction) describes the use of visuals, the rationale for the design and development of visuals for learning, and describes how visuals affect understanding and learning in your audience.
- Chapter 2 (Visual Stimuli) outlines the kinds of visuals and degrees of visualization.
- Chapter 3 (Visual Thinking) provides the tools for visualizing a wide range of information. This section also contains a number of exercises that provide you with an opportunity to practice visual thinking and design.
- Chapter 4 (Visual Design Considerations) presents a series of questions you can use to evaluate the visuals you produce.
- Chapter 5 (Field Testing and Rendering Visuals) outlines the process of designing visuals in the context of creating a lesson or presentation.
- The Appendix contains: a glossary, forms, checklists, an annotated bibliography and an index.

Format

This book may be used in three ways:

- As a general orientation to the creation of visuals
- As a "how to" manual to support visual product development
- As a reference guide for those who have completed it once and want to refresh themselves.

Notes and Hints

Notes and hints appear in the margin.

Exercises and Alternative Solutions to Exercise

The book includes exercises to complete. Exercises appear in shaded boxes. After completing an exercise, the reader is encouraged to compare his or her answers with other possible alternatives, which are presented at the end of each chapter.

Forms and Checklists

This book includes the following materials that will assist you in developing effective visuals:

- Forms are for use in planning, designing and developing visuals.
- Checklists enable you to evaluate visuals.
- Blank forms and checklists are presented in the Appendix. You may copy these for use in developing your course presentation.

VISUAL COMMUNICATING

Preface   iv

How to Use This Book   v

CHAPTER 1   Introduction   3

Verbalization vs. Visualization   5

Visualization as a New Language   6

Visualization as a Process   7

CHAPTER 2   Visual Stimuli   11

Kinds of Visuals   11

Degrees of Visualization   18

Type I	Reader Frame	20
Type II	Emphasized Reader Frame	20
Type III	Reader Frame with Visual Cues to Meaning	22
Type IV	Verbal/Visual Balanced Frame	23
Type V	Pictorial or Graphic Symbol Frame with Verbal Cues to Meaning	24
Type VI	Emphasized Pictorial or Graphic Symbol Frame	25
Type VII	Pictorial or Graphic Symbol Frame	26

Combining Verbal and Visual Types in Your Presentation   27

Factors Affecting the Kind and Degree of Visualization to Choose   29

Alternative Solutions to Exercises in Chapter 2   24

CHAPTER 3   Visual Thinking   37

Visualizing Numerical Data   39

Types of Graphs   39
- Circle Graph   39
- Line Graph   40
- Bar Graph   41
- Pictorial Graph   43
- Map or Area Graph   44

The Titling of Graphs   46

Visualizing Facts, Directions, and Processes   49

Facts   49

Directions   50

Processes   53

Visualizing Concepts	**54**
Visible Concepts	54
•Plans and Organizational Charts	54
•Maps	56
•Chronologies	58
Invisible Concepts	59
•Generalizations	59
•Theories	61
•Feelings or Attitudes	62
Conclusion	**62**
Alternative Solutions to Exercises in Chapter 3	63
CHAPTER 4 Visual Design Considerations	**79**
Clarity	**79**
Progressive disclosure	84
Establishing and zooming in on the subject	85
Panning or tilting	85
Simple animation	86
Summing Up: Clarity	86
Unity	**88**
Summing Up: Unity	93
Imagination	**94**
Summing Up: Imagination	97
Conclusion	**97**
Revised Visuals for Clarity, Unity, and Imagination Exercises	99
CHAPTER 5 Field Testing and Rendering Visuals	**105**
Choosing Your Best Alternative	**105**
Rendering Your Visual Presentation	**106**
Appendix	**109**
Glossary	111
Forms and Checklists	115
Annotated Bibliography	123
Index	145

About the Author:

Ralph Wileman is a native Buckeye turned Tarheel.

He matriculated at Otterbein College, Kent State University, Parsons School of Design, and Teachers College, Columbia University.

Teaching has been a major vocation, starting with Lakeview High School in Winter Garden Florida, to Fredonia College, University of Hawaii, and decades at the University of North Carolina.

Graphic arts, optical toys and illusionary devices, training visual thinkers, working on health learning material in Africa and Asia, folk art, multi-image production, directing the graduate study of instructional designers are major threads of his professional life.

Watching Laura Hayes and John Howard mature is his greatest pleasure.

Introduction

In learning environments throughout education, the visual elements of courses, lessons, and presentations play an important role in learning. Well-conceived and rendered visuals help your audience understand and retain information. This guide can enhance your ability to conceptualize and develop visuals that effectively fulfill the objectives being taught.

It is your job as a lesson developer to conceptualize the visuals. You do not have to be an artist to do this. Artists can render your concepts, but only you – who best understands the learning objectives involved – can design the visuals that will produce the most effective learning.

Visuals are used in many learning environments: the traditional classroom, satellite education, computer-based training, interactive videodisc, videotape, and print materials from text to handouts. They all can accommodate visual messages. Visuals can be used effectively to teach facts, data, directions, processes, and invisible concepts that are often complex or elusive. All learning objectives can be facilitated through visualization. We learn in a variety of ways. We gather a majority of our information through our eyes. We learn from observation of the real world and from man-made visuals of all types from 14th century paintings to 3-D models of chemical structures. In a typical lecture, the teacher uses overhead transparencies or other media primarily to project words on the screen. This visual presentation of verbal information does not utilize the rich array of ways people learn visually. Heavy emphasis on text-based visuals has proven to be an ineffective teaching methodology. This guide will focus the reader's attention on the visual aspect of the educational process.

The next time you are on an airplane, notice the emergency card. (See Figures 1 and 2.) What will it look like, Figure 1 or Figure 2? Might it be a combination of Figure 1 and Figure 2? Why do the airlines use highly visual representation to communicate such important information? As you study Figure 1 and Figure 2, note that you "read" both of them. You must be literate to read either. Someone who is not literate would not be able to process the information in either figure. Figure 1 would be a problem because it must be "read" from left to right and top to

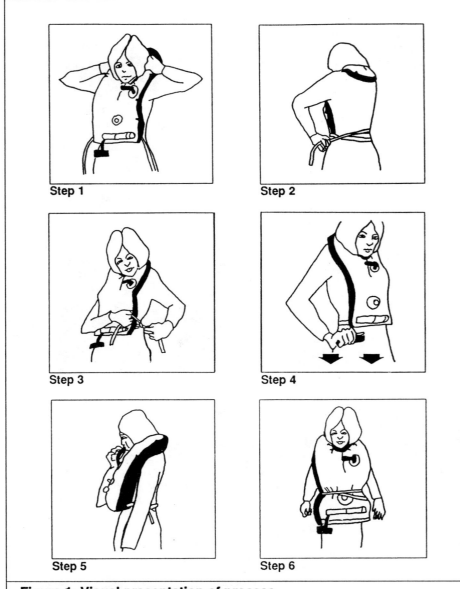

Figure 1: Visual presentation of process

Step 1:
Your life jacket is under your seat. Remove jacket from case and place over head.

Step 2:
Pull tapes firmly downwards. Pass tapes around waist, cross behind back.

Step 3:
Pull tapes firmly downwards. at the left side of the jacket.

Step 4:
After leaving the aircraft inflate life jacket automatically by pulling red knob at bottom sharply dowwards.

Step 5:
If the life jacket fails to inflate, blow into the mouth piece at front of jacket at neck level.

Step 6:
You are now prepared to float.

Figure 2: Verbal presentation of process

bottom. It also uses conventions of visual literacy that we take for granted, such as the use of arrows to show movement in Step 4. Figure 2 would be a problem for obvious reasons.

By becoming more competent in the design and development of visuals, you will eliminate the inefficient and frustrating trial-and-error approach that too frequently occurs between a lesson designer and the graphic artist who is rendering the visuals. Traditionally, graphic artists spend much of their time attempting to understand what a lesson designer wants in a given visual. After making a "best guess," the artists render the visual. The lesson designer often reports that a visual must be redone a number of times until the artist gets it right.

You can avoid this trial-and-error approach if you, as the lesson designer, give the artist sketches that clearly outline the images and information needed in a given visual. The primary goal of the guide is to help you do just that, enabling you to minimize unnecessary revisions and to create visuals that work. This guide helps you to plan what learners will see, just as you plan carefully what they will hear or read. You will learn how to translate your learning objectives into visual concepts and then how to assess the visual conceptualization. And, if you have access to a graphic artist (or illustrator or photographer, etc.), the guide will help you make good use of your artist's special skills, which is to render clear visual images in a given medium.

Your level of competence in drawing is not important. Your contribution is to define learning objectives and structure for lessons, and to translate verbal information into effective visual concepts. The graphic artist's contribution is to provide production expertise during the rendering stage. You decide what is to be seen; someone else will produce it.

Today there is a wide variety of media and media delivery systems for delivering visual images. The electronic/digital communications field is one of the fastest growing and changing facets of society. All indications point to more and better visual media and media delivery systems for us to use to facilitate learning. The resources are here; can we use them to help the learner understand and remember? Yes, we can!

Visual images offer several advantages over verbal communications. They can:

Present more information in a given amount of space

Simplify complex concepts

Clarify pieces of an abstract, language-based concept

Serve as advance organizers of information

Most importantly, research suggests that visual images increase learning retention, which is one of the primary goals of educators.

Verbalization vs. Visualization

We communicate with each other about our world and our responses to it. Objects, processes, data, concepts, theories, feelings – the components of our experience – are described by means of the spoken and written word.

We can also communicate our experiences visually. However, more often than not, we feel more comfortable using verbal rather than visual communication. The reason for this may be that we are trained in the use of verbalization from our earliest days. The verbalization skills of writing and reading are presently the foundation of learning; the majority of the primary school day is spent teaching children to read, or using the spoken or written word to teach subject matter.

This ability to share knowledge through verbal techniques is a skill of great benefit to humans; its value cannot be reasonably disputed in or out of the classroom. However, verbalization is not the only way we can learn or communicate. The purpose of this guide is to demonstrate the importance of visualization in the learning process.

Despite the fact that we see our world more than we speak or read of it, we are rarely trained in the use of visual techniques to communicate messages. In fact, we are taught to express our visual experiences verbally or to transfer them into written words. As a result, our use of visuals to communicate has been limited.

There are three major reasons for using visualization to communicate information:

1. A visual message can get the audience's attention. A dynamic visual display demands attention. Gaining attention is the first step in communicating.

Three major reasons for using visualization to communicate information:
1. **A visual message can get the audience's attention.**
2. **A visual message can be efficient.**
3. **A visual message can be effective.**

2. A visual message can be efficient. A visual display can communicate quickly and boldly. Thus it can hasten comprehension of the message.

3. A visual message can be effective. A visual display has the capacity to produce the desired outcome. If the communicator/teacher wants the audience/learner to focus on a particular aspect of a comprehensive message, the visual display can be designed with that specific focus in mind. Visuals help people remember the message.

In recent years, the rise of television and sophisticated media delivery systems has placed a new emphasis on visual communications. However, there is still a dearth of truly imaginative and appropriate visual learning materials.

Of the materials that do exist, many are poorly conceptualized visual messages. Even a visual message can be confusing if it is poorly designed! This guide is intended to challenge you to generate original, well-conceived visualization that enhances the learning process.

Visualization as a New Language

Communication requires a message sender and a message receiver. The fact that the receiver says "I see," when the message is clear – or "Show me an example," "Draw me a picture," or "Describe it for me" when more information is required – all indicate a desire to learn through visual communication. Today's audiences readily accept visual messages.

As an educational message designer, you should therefore be willing to exploit visual communications in the educational environment – either by selecting the most effective visual materials the marketplace has to offer or by developing new materials when necessary.

Visualization, like verbalization, generates a language from its elements, structure, and uses. However, if this language is to offer the viewer more than just a nonverbal image, it must present a visual message the viewer can understand. Communication can be judged successful only when it conveys the information it sets out to convey. This is as true for visual modes as it is for verbal modes.

Educational message designers – be they course developers, instructors, audio-visual specialists, or communicators in any field – must be familiar with the methods used to interpret and present various types of information visually. The audience, regardless of their age and level, have learned to "read" the language of visual messages just as they have learned to read verbal messages. Both designers and the audience must be as literate visually as they are verbally.

We know that visualization can be applied to a wide range of messages. The following list clarifies the range of educational messages that visuals can be used to represent:
1. Concrete facts (e.g., the major types of energy resources)
2. Directions (e.g., the steps a learner goes through to service a computer). Examples here are "how-to-do-its."
3. Processes (e.g., the steps that industry goes through to make steel). Examples help the learner understand a procedure without necessarily having to perform it.
4. A bit of data (e.g., the 1990 sales figure for all microcomputers)
5. Comparative data (e.g., comparing children, young adults, and mature adults in their use of electronic toothbrushes)
6. Data recorded over time (e.g., the average rainfall in Maine for the past 100 years)
7. An organizational structure (e.g., the U.S. State Department)
8. Places (e.g., a map of Vatican City)
9. Chronologies (e.g., the history of human ground transportation, from the sled to the automobile)
10. Generalization (e.g., the invest-

ment potential of a nation)
11. A theory (e.g., Maslow's Holistic-Dynamic theory)
12. Feelings or attitudes. Examples here would be similar to those in categories 1 through 11, but would also reflect emotions such as cooperation, love, sorrow, etc. The examples would communicate both information and a point of view.

The enormous amount of information our society needs to communicate, coupled with the wide range of media alternatives to display that information, makes for complex choices on the part of educational designers. Education has moved quite slowly and cautiously in the use of visualization.

As early as 1897, the educator John Dewey emphasized the importance of using visual images in the instructional process:

"I believe that the image is the great instrument in instruction. What a student gets out of any subject presented to him is simply the images which he himself forms with regard to it."

"I believe that if nine tenths of the energy at present directed toward making students learn certain things were spent in seeing to it that the student was forming proper images, the work of instruction would be infinitely facilitated."

"I believe much of the time and attention now given to the preparation and presentation of lessons might be more wisely and profitably expended in training the student's power of imagery and in seeing to it that he is continually forming definite, vivid, and growing images of the various subjects with which he comes in contact in his experience."

In 1954, the educator Edgar Dale – one of the early advocates of audio-visual techniques – summarized the communicator's role in relation to visual communication: "It is our task as teachers to make [visual symbols] rich and strong, with meaning for the student."

Today, you are charged with the task of helping students learn through the visual images available in sophisticated electronic learning environments.

The range of educational messages that visuals can be used to represent:

1. **Concrete facts**
2. **Directions**
3. **Processes**
4. **Bits of data**
5. **Comparative data**
6. **Data recorded over time**
7. **Organizational structures**
8. **Places**
9. **Chronologies**
10. **Generalizations**
11. **Theories**
12. **Feelings or attitudes**

Visualization as a Process

In the context of this guide, visualization is considered primarily as a process and secondarily as a product. You, as a lesson developer, must intellectually grapple with a message before arriving at a visual solution.

Designing educational materials in any medium calls for a great deal of thought. Many articles in education periodicals have titles such as "A Quick and Easy Way to Make_____," or "You Too Can Have Fun Making_____." By emphasizing the product rather than the process, such articles give a misleading view of how materials should be developed.

It is conceptualization – not the rendering – of the materials that makes an effective educational product. Conceptualization is the intellectual process you use to visualize messages. Rarely is it a process that is easy, quick, or fun, although it is often satisfying.

Good visual materials created for learning can take hours to conceptualize and more hours to render.

Conceptualizing and rendering are two different and difficult tasks. Conceptualization, the intellectual task, is the focus of this guide. Rendering, the task of producing the final visual, is the domain of a graphic artist. It is not the purpose of this guide to train you to become a graphic artist. However, it is important to understand the principle used by a graphic artist – such as layout, color, and choice of typeface when designing visuals.

Visual message design requires a great deal of mental and physical action; it depends on intelligent decision-making at every stage of the process. However, even though it can be an arduous task, it is not a thankless one. Quite the contrary; creating new visual educational materials can be challenging and – when the learner shows evidence of learning – very rewarding.

Although some of what educational designers do is instructive or intuitive, much of what they do is based on skills learned by studying and practicing the visualization process. One function of this guide, therefore, is to stimulate or rekindle your instinctive ability to visualize. Another function is to give you – as both a lesson developer and an educational message designer – the knowledge and practice you will need to create attention-getting, effective, and efficient educational messages.

Notes

Visual Stimuli

We are surrounded by objects. Some are a part of the natural environment and some are man-made. Objects have always been central to our lives, and our communication with one another has always been largely concerned with concrete things, with matter, with nouns.

Early humans carved or painted on cave walls the things they knew – things such as the family, animals, and their natural environment. Those early renderings were used to record facts and to communicate ideas. To be effective, the images had to be "read" (seen, understood, and interpreted as intended), just as we read words on the printed page today.

For the most part these images were drawn realistically and were easy to understand. Some of these early images developed into more abstract shapes that evolved into the letters used for written communication.

This chapter has three parts:
- The first part focuses on developing an understanding of the kinds of visuals you can use.
- The second part describes the degrees of visualization you can employ.
- The concluding part briefly looks at the factors influencing your choice of kind and degree of visualization to employ as you make visuals for teaching.

Kinds of Visuals

The representation of one object by another object is a symbol. Objects, actions, or processes can be represented by a symbol or a series of symbols. There are three major ways to represent objects – as pictorial symbols, graphic symbols, or verbal symbols. These categories are illustrated in Figure 3; refer to that figure as you read the following definitions.

Pictorial symbols are produced as photographs, illustrations, or drawings. All of these are attempts to represent the object or thing as a highly realistic and concrete symbol. The viewers should easily be able to translate a pictorial symbol to a real-world example. That is, after looking at a pictorial symbol of a modem, students should be able to recognize a real modem in the work place.

Graphic symbols (see Figure 4) are constructed in a variety of ways.

Figure 3. Ways to represent an object

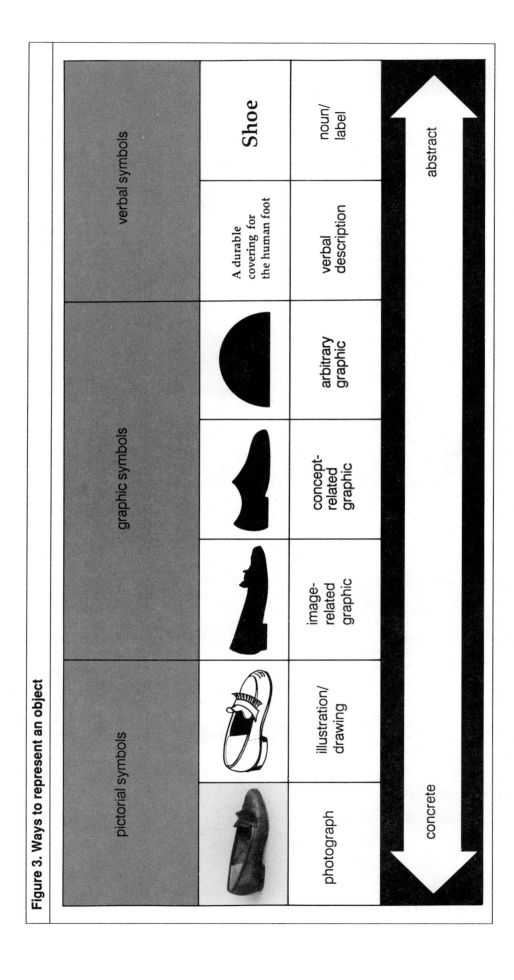

The English artist Rudolf Modley suggested three major categories of graphic symbols:

• *Image-related graphics*
These can best be characterized as silhouettes or profiles of the object. The object has no surface detail, but remains quite recognizable.

• *Concept-related graphics*
These look like the object, but have less detail than image-related graphics. Concept-related graphics are the essence of the object; they are a stylized version of the real thing.

• *Arbitrary graphics*
These are abstract symbols for an object. At times, arbitrary graphics take the form of geometric shapes. They are constructed out of the designer's imagination and, as their name implies, may be visually unrelated to the object.

Verbal symbols are single words or whole sentences. We either use nouns to label objects or string words together to define or describe an object. Actions too are represented with verbal symbols. Verbal symbols can be understood only by people who understand the language used to describe the objects or actions.

The three major symbol groupings help cluster the range of ways we represent objects visually. This range runs from concrete to abstract representation. Pictorial symbols are usually highly realistic and very concrete. Graphic symbols may or may not be easy to read. Verbal symbols come to us in many languages; when we hear or read a language we do not know, we become aware of just how abstract verbal symbols are.

We use pictorial, graphic, and verbal symbols in a wide range of media. The choice of symbols is directly related to our major objective, which is to communicate specific information that is suitable to our audience's ability and inter-

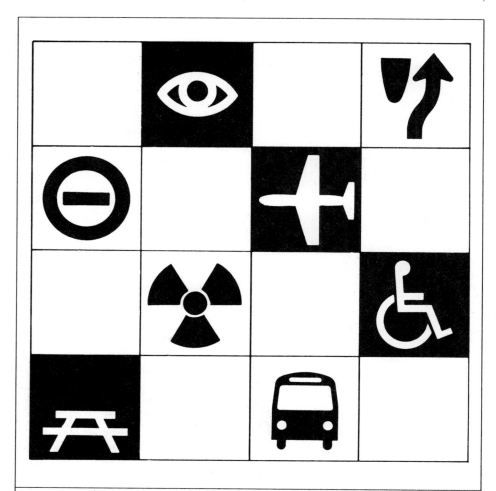

Figure 4. Examples of graphic symbols

ests. As the course developer, you should become equally adept at designing symbols in all categories, from concrete to abstract. It is important to interweave pictorial, graphic, and verbal symbols to make your educational messages more effective.

You have considerable technological support available to produce symbols at the concrete end of the continuum. This support takes the form of 35mm cameras and video cameras – as well as accomplished artists who can render highly realistic paintings and drawings.

Likewise, people have considerable experience and ability in producing verbal symbols at the abstract end of the continuum. We are constantly using and abusing verbal symbols in the educational environment.

We seem to need the most help in inventing images to use in the graphic symbol range on the continuum (see Figure 3). Henry Dreyfus has compiled a significant reference tool to help us see the range of existing symbols. His *Symbol Sourcebook* will acquaint you with the breadth and depth of the graphic symbols already in use.

Often, however, our task is to invent or design a new graphic symbol. Exercise I gives you practice in this activity.

A good source of inspiration in the development of graphic symbols is *Form and Communication*. In this book, Diethelm gives examples of geometric mathematical approaches to graphic design-making. The results of following his directions can lead you to designs with infinite variation.

For additional inspiration regard-

ing the design of graphic symbols, make it a practice to study the logos of major corporations and organizations. Look also at the "Trademarks and Symbols" section of each *Graphis Annual*. Although many of the examples in that design periodical are logotypes rather than graphic symbols, most of them attempt to communicate the function or ambience of an entire company or organization. The vast majority of these symbols are bold, flat, and graphic. They also represent the efforts of the world's leading graphic designers.

When you evaluate a symbol you have designed, ask the fundamental question: Does the symbol communicate? In other words, does your audience or learner read and understand the symbol, then interpret it as intended? If the answer is no, you should redesign the symbol. At another level, ask: "Is the symbol well-designed?" Here, taste and opinion play a strong role. Be prepared to deal with both logical and emotional responses to your work.

You can deal with logical responses by changing or redesigning your symbols. For instance, look at a "before" example (Figure 5); a logical criticism might be that the human shape is clumsy and disproportional. You can rework your design to resolve that problem as shown in the "after" example (Figure 5). Sometimes you are given criticism that is emotional and based primarily on personal whim or fancy. For example, look at Figure 6. This symbol has been designed to stand for health centers (an arbitrary graphic symbol). An emotional criticism might be that the shape looks too much like a snowflake. Do not

Note:
*See Appendix for complete references to **Symbol Sourcebook, Form and Communication**, and other books described in this guide.*

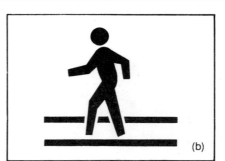

(a)   (b)

Figure 5. "Before" (a) and "After" (b) reworking design

Exercise 1

Making Up Symbols

The visual to the right is incomplete. There are three graphics symbols missing. Fill in each blank space with an appropriate symbol of your own design. Work on a separate sheet of paper. After you have created three rough sketches for each symbol, transfer your best sketch to the chart on the right.

(Note: use a blunt-tip black felt marker to achieve a solid rather than line-oriented image. Create graphic symbols that are bold and flat like the ones already printed on the chart.)

pictorial symbols		graphic symbols			verbal symbols	
photograph	illustration	image-related	concept-related	arbitrary	definition	noun
					optical instrument that ENLARGES minute objects	MICROSCOPE
					small, furry, feline animal	cat
					A woody plant with a single main stem or trunk	Tree
					A shelter occupied by a small number of people	House

15

Hint:
Test your ideas with both peers and people who are representative of your intended audience. Your peers, because they are well-versed in instructional design, will give you educationally sound criticism. The audience group will let you know, on the most direct level, if your ideas work for them.

rework your design because of this response – perhaps every pronged and round shape looks like a snowflake to your critic.

Change your design only when criticism is logical and seems valid; hold your ground when criticism is illogical or invalid.

Remember, all graphic symbols must be identifiable (recognized by the audience.) Abstract symbols should be unique and must not be confused with other well-known arbitrary symbols.

A rich and varied range of visuals can be used to represent your ideas. This is evident when you view Figure 7. The range of visuals, from left to right, has many points along the horizontal continuum – from concrete to abstract. As you may have already discovered, there is also a vertical dimension to this continuum that adds further richness and variety to your choice.

There is more than one photograph to use, more than one illustration, more than one image-related graphic, and so on.

In fact, there are infinite ways to represent objects and things at each point along the continuum. The rendering style of the illustrator, the graphic artist, or the photographer will come into play in your choice of one visual over another. As the course developer or instructional designer, you must specify the type of visual that will best meet your instructional needs.

Becoming familiar with the alternative ways to represent objects is fundamental to instructional design. These alternatives must be willingly explored and pondered as you go about designing messages. Exercise II on page 18 will give you practice in developing designs for an object in all the various forms discussed in this chapter– from concrete to abstract.

Figure 6. Arbitrary graphics

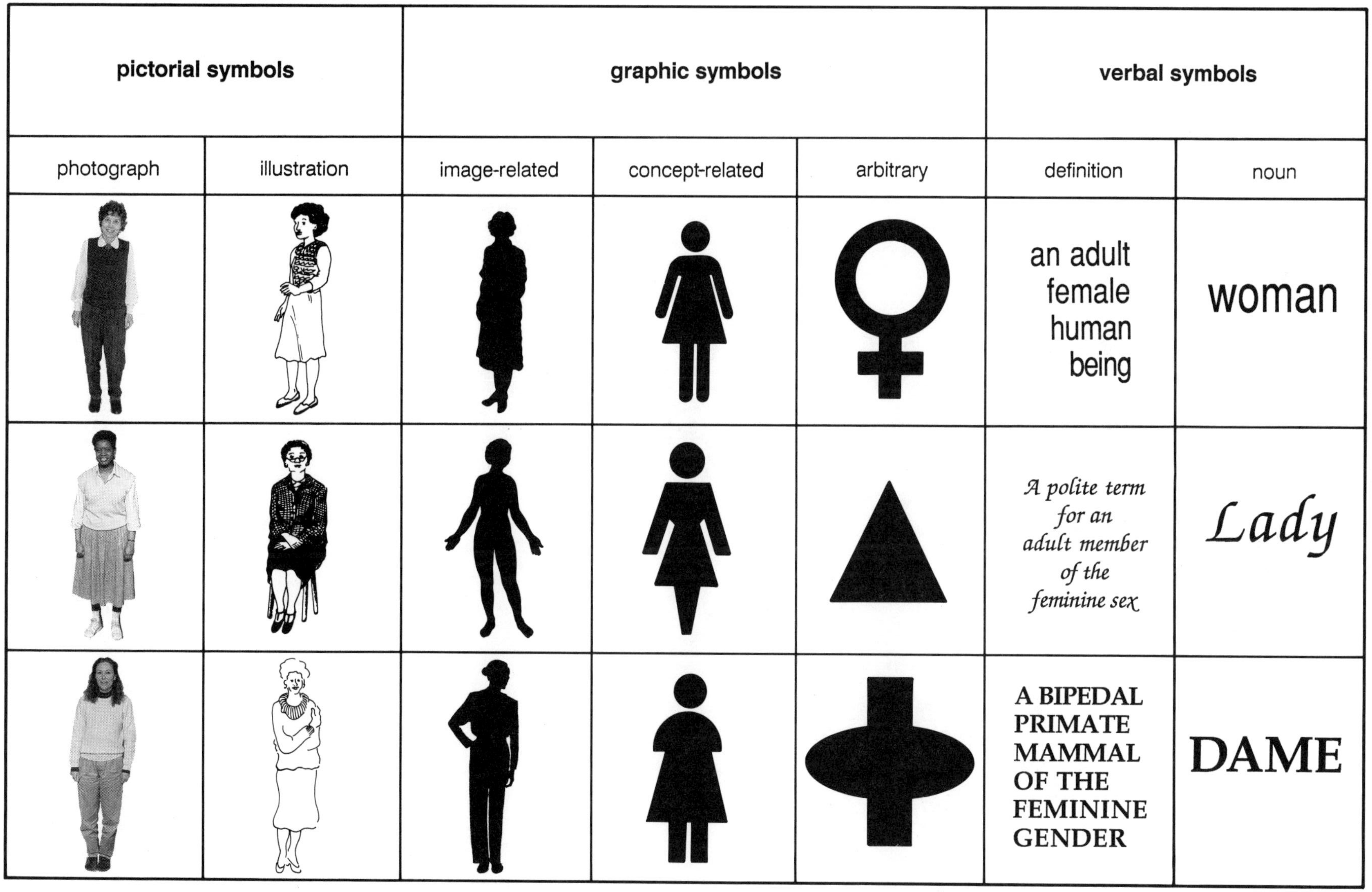

pictorial symbols		graphic symbols			verbal symbols	
photograph	illustration	image-related	concept-related	arbitrary	definition	noun
				♀	an adult female human being	woman
				◀	A polite term for an adult member of the feminine sex	Lady
					A BIPEDAL PRIMATE MAMMAL OF THE FEMININE GENDER	DAME

Figure 7. The variety of possible ways to represent a single concept

Exercise II

Making a picture series

Select a photograph of an object from a magazine (or photograph an object of your choice). Using that photograph as the first visual in your series, design a picture series of the object that includes each of the following:

1. Photograph
2. Illustration/drawing
3. Image-related graphic
4. Concept-related graphic
5. Arbitrary graphic
6. Definition/description
7. Noun label

Sample answers to this exercise are shown on page 33.

Hint:

Your solution to Exercise II could be mounted on a board and displayed on the wall of your office to remind yourself how to represent objects as you go about the business of visual message design.

Degrees of Visualization

Spoken and written words play a significant part in our communication. When your message is communicated in a form other than the spoken or written word – i.e., in a visual form using slides, computer graphics, video, overhead transparencies, or film – you are often dealing with complex relationships between words (verbal images) and pictures (visual images). Part of this complexity stems from the fact that there are many types of relationships between verbal and visual images.

This discussion focuses on the verbal and the visual images that an audience or individual learner might see projected on a screen or in print. It does not include the words, spoken by an instructor or narrator, that accompany the projected images.

You often find educational materials that are called visual aids to learning – just because they are in projectable formats. Observe these materials carefully: In many cases learning is not aided visually. You would not call a page of type in a book a visual aid; yet once it is photographed and projected on a screen, it is usually *called* a visual aid.

Projecting words on a screen is not necessarily right or wrong. However, visual aids worthy of projection are distinctly different from the spoken or printed word; they are more likely to include photography, illustrations, or graphic symbols and only a few significant words.

Figure 8 shows a way to organize the relationship of verbal and visual images along a continuum. This verbal/visual continuum we call the **degrees of visualization**. It is represented in this guide by seven different types of visuals – types that range from the purely verbal (Type I) to the purely visual (Type VII). The following discussion describes each of these types in some detail.

Hint:

A copy of Figure 8 could be mounted on a board and displayed on the wall of your office to remind you of the degrees of visualization available for your use. Consult this chart frequently as you go about the business of designing your visual messages.

How Visual Is Your Visual-Aid?

Type I
READER Frame (pure verbal)

Type II
EMPHASIZED READER Frame

Type III
Reader Frame with VISUAL CUES to meaning

Type IV
Verbal/Visual BALANCED Frame

Type V
Pictorial or Graphic Symbol Frame with VERBAL CUES to meaning

Type VI
EMPHASIZED PICTORIAL or GRAPHIC Symbol Frame

Type VII
PICTORIAL or GRAPHIC Symbol Frame (pure visual)

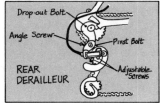

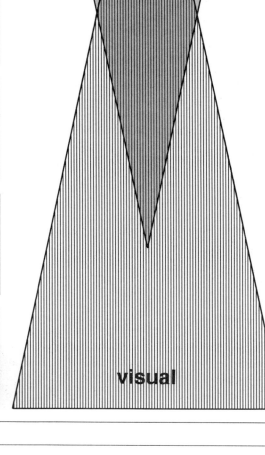

Figure 8. The verbal/visual continuum

Type I – Reader Frame

This purely verbal presentation closely resembles the printed page. In order to comprehend the message, the viewer must be verbally literate (see Figure 9). As the designer, you can affect the message through the choice of typeface, layout of type, and the use of color for the background and/or the type. Reader frames are often short titles, headings, or lists of words. They are used to outline ideas that will be presented in subsequent frames, to summarize or review preceding frames, or to condense the instructor's narrative.

LAST NAME IN THE 1985
LONDON TELEPHONE BOOK:

<u>Zzzzzzz Coffee Shop</u>

in GRAY'S INN ROAD

Figure 9. Reader Frame

Type II – Emphasized Reader Frame

This presentation is still verbal, but adds an element we will call "emphasis." Emphasis can be applied to reader frames in a variety of ways. Sometimes emphasis is strictly decorative, as in Figure 10, where words are bordered with a filigree pattern. This example may be attractive and well-designed, but we should ask the question, "Does it help the viewer understand the message better?" Probably not. However, this technique can attract or capture the viewer's attention; it probably encourages the viewer to read the message. Thus it may serve a useful instructional purpose. At other times, typographic emphasis (e.g., **boldface**, *italics*, or change of typeface) can be used to accentuate part of the message. Accentuation helps focus the viewer's attention. For example, by placing an asterisk beside two items out of five, we accentuate those items (see Figure 11).

Decorative or typographic emphasis techniques include:

- Changing the typeface for key words
- Using all upper-case or all lower-case letters for key words
- Changing type size
- Using color
- Using a star, asterisk, or check mark beside key words

THE MAINFRAME

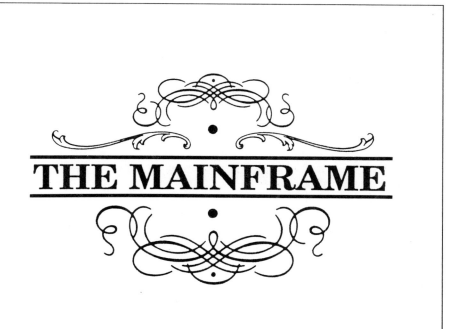

Figure 10. Emphasized Reader Frame (decorative)

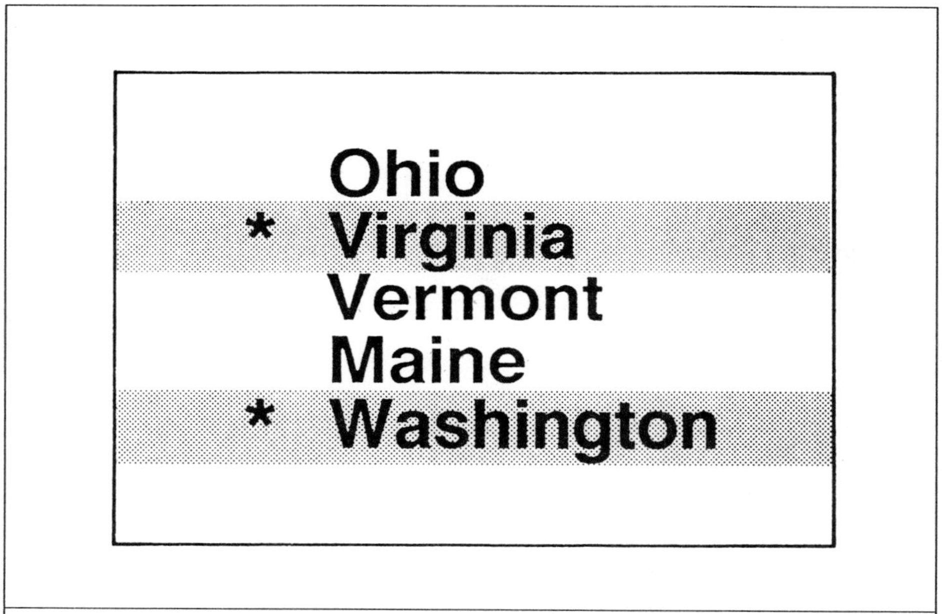
Ohio
* Virginia
Vermont
Maine
* Washington

Figure 11. Emphasized Reader Frame (directing attention)

Hint:
When adding emphasis to a frame, remember that too much emphasis can actually detract from your message and create confusion. For example, using a different color for each letter of a word you want to emphasize may end up forcing the viewer to focus elsewhere in order to avoid the difficulty of reading a multicolored word. Be sure your choice of technique adds not only emphasis but also clarity to your visual.

Type III – Reader Frame with Visual Cues to Meaning

This presentation is verbal, but it adds pictorial or graphic symbols that help communicate the message. In Figure 12, the words in the cloud tell the viewer a bit more about the location of airborne pollution. Figure 13 explains the subject of the presentation verbally, and also gives a visual cue to the relationship between the two elements: development affects population, and population affects development. In short, development and population mesh like gears.

In a Type III presentation, viewers receive part of the message from what they see, rather than having to rely totally on what they read. This treatment is designed to direct and hold the viewers' attention, while it underscores the meaning.

Figure 12. Reader Frame with visual cues to meaning (pollution)

Figure 13. Reader Frame with visual cues to meaning (gears)

Type IV – Verbal/Visual Balanced Frame

This type of presentation is balanced; it offers the viewer the opportunity to receive the information as a verbal message, a visual message, or a message that combines the two. For example, Figure 14 communicates the concept of the rain cycle as a verbal message, a visual message, or a visual/verbal combination.

In a Type IV visual, the learner can understand the message by either reading the pictures or reading the words. The frame is visually and verbally redundant.

Note that the cyclical layout of the words (as opposed to a linear list) also contributes to the understanding of the message. A judicious use of words, combined with clear, meaningful graphics, can intrigue the viewer and provoke a great deal of inquiry into the meaning of the message.

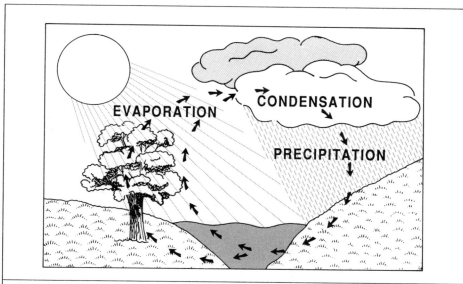

Figure 14. Verbal/Visual balanced frame

Type V – Pictorial or Graphic Symbol Frame with Verbal Cues to Meaning

At the end of the continuum the visualization of the message becomes primary; words are used only as landmarks or to label new or exotic phenomena. For example, Figure 15 depicts the location of three important glands in the body. The drawing uses few words, but they serve to orient the viewer. A Type V visual communicates a com- plex idea in visual terms, and the words help to clarify the message. A Type V visual is appropriate to use in the representation of numerical data, where the message is visualized and words are used only to orient the viewer (see Figure 16). Although the viewer must be able to read in order to understand this graph, the major aspect of this message comes from "reading" or interpreting the visual side of the presentation. The viewer needs to be visually literate to under- stand the data.

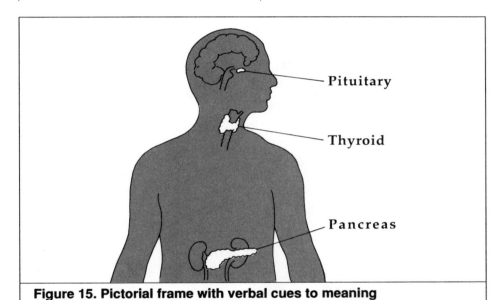

Figure 15. Pictorial frame with verbal cues to meaning

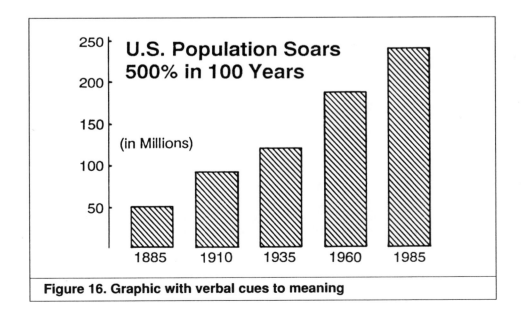

Figure 16. Graphic with verbal cues to meaning

Type VI – Emphasized Pictorial or Graphic Symbol Frame

No words are included in this type of presentation. For example, in Figure 17 it is clear that two elements are the focus of our attention. The viewer must be able to "read" the emphasizing technique – in this case, the cloud shapes and the arrows that emphasize how airborne particles affect workers.

Pictorial or graphic emphasis techniques include:
• Using arrows to point out, signal direction, or show flow
• Using a circle to isolate an aspect of the visual message
• Using a bold or delicate style to emphasize an aspect of the image
• Using screens, textures, or colors around the element to be emphasized
• Enlarging an aspect as if it were under a magnifying glass
• Use of grouping or relative position

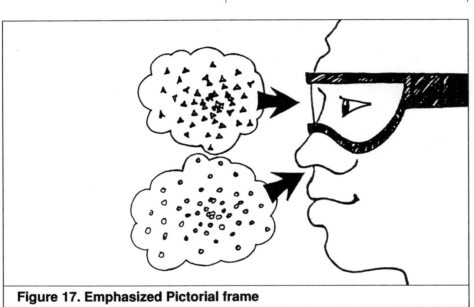

Figure 17. Emphasized Pictorial frame

Type VII – Pictorial or Graphic Symbol Frame

This presentation is purely visual. Photographs, detailed illustrations, simple graphics, and geometric shapes are used to communicate the message. For example, a photograph of an offline editing switcher (Figure 18) tells the viewer something about video editing equipment. Likewise, the illustration of the lab worker (Figure 19) is pure visual information.

Type VII visuals are used most often in slide and video presentations. The camera is used to photographically record an event, a place, or an artist's rendered illustration. The distinguishing feature is the style or technique of the photographer or the renderer. For example, if the subject to be communicated is tongue-and-groove construction, the quality of the delivery is directly related to the skill of the photographer or rendering artist.

Hint:

When selecting photographers, illustrators, or graphic artists to render your visuals, be sure to view examples of their work. These examples can help you to assess how their skill and style will match your requirements.

Figure 18. Photograph

Figure 19. Illustration

Combining Verbal and Visual Types in Your Presentation

As you go about conceptualizing visuals to fit all kinds of content – with the eventual goal of producing slides, computer graphics, videos, exhibits, and the like – you should make an effort to include all degrees of visualization. In other words, try to use all seven types of verbal/visual image relationships presented in this section.

The real challenge for designers is to produce an interesting combination of the various verbal and visual types, with emphasis on Types III, IV, and V. These three types provide a blend of words and pictorial or graphic images. For most audiences, this mix of types – including various degrees of visualization – is the most helpful in terms of learning.

A survey of existing slides, foils, and computer graphics is likely to reveal a preponderance of Type I and Type VII presentations. Most slide presentations are either "reader" frames, or else photographs or illustrations of persons, places, or things. In this rather "easy" solution to visual design, the substance of the message is carried by narration.

Perhaps you have heard this approach, called the "illustrated lecture." In most cases, the audience will not miss much of the message if the lecturer forgets to bring the visuals to the presentation. The visuals are usually not nearly as important as the narration. The lecturer could speak without the visuals, but could the visuals be presented without the lecturer? Probably not.

The inadequate use of visualization in presentations could be overcome if the presentations were conceptualized on storyboards rather than on typewriters. A storyboard is a verbal and visual plan (see Figure 20). The use of a storyboard encourages you to visualize during the conceptualization stage of planning. Successful educational media producers take full advantage of this planning tool (see Figure 21).

The traditional planning technique – script writing – emphasizes only the verbal aspect of the presentation, whereas the storyboard takes into account both verbal and visual learning modes. The verbal portion can also be the narration in an audiovisual presentation or the spoken message accompanying the visual in a classroom.

A well-conceived presentation, no matter what the format, demands that a significant part of the message be communicated visually. How much or how little you need to visualize depends upon the kind of message to be communicated. The various kinds of messages will be described in the next chapter.

Perform Exercise III to test your ability to classify the degrees of visualization into various types of verbal/visual presentations.

Figure 20. Storyboard cards

Exercise III

Classifying Visuals by Degree

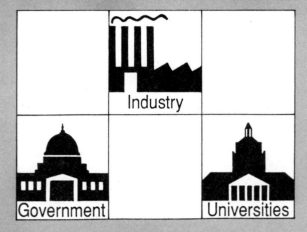

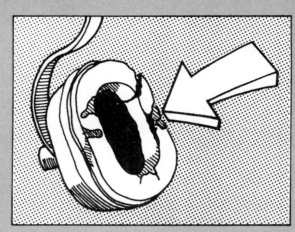

AREAS OF MANAGEMENT SUPPORT

- **GUIDANCE**
- **ASSISTANCE**
- **MOTIVATION**
- **ORIENTATION**

Classify the four examples above as to the following types:

Type I — Reader Frame (pure verbal)
Type II — Emphasized Reader Frame
Type III — Reader Frame with Visuals Cues to Meaning
Type IV — Verbal/Visual Balanced Frame
Type V — Pictorial or Graphic Symbol Frame with Verbal Cues to Meaning
Type VI — Emphasized Pictorial or Graphic Symbol Frame
Type VII — Pictorial or Graphic Symbol Frame (pure visual)

The correct answers are on page 34.

Figure 21. A storyboard conference

Factors Affecting the Kind and Degree of Visualization to Choose

An educator must understand the many kinds of visuals available and must know that a visual aid can be classified according to its degree of visualization. In designing a visual presentation or visual support for a lecture or discussion, it is important to establish what **kind** of visual to choose, and what **degree** of visualization to employ.

There are six factors that influence the choice of kind and degree:

- Instructional objectives
- Audience characteristics
- Content analysis
- Medium employed
- Time and resources
- Ability to think visually

Instructional objectives influence the kind and degree of visual to employ. For example, if it is your objective that the learners be able to name products when they see them being operated in certain work areas, then the kinds of visuals should be full-color photographs of products in various work places. Two degrees of visuals should be used in this learning sequence. First, you should use Type V – Pictorial with Verbal Cues to Meaning – to teach the material. Later, you should use Type VII – Pure Visuals – to test their knowledge.

Audience characteristics also influence your selection. For example, if your audience is adults in a public health clinic, the kind of visual should be realistic drawings, not cartoons; the latter are often associated with presentations for children and therefore may be offensive. The degree of visualization should be highly visual (Types VI and VII), with no words on the screen, since some adults may have difficulty reading.

A **content analysis** of what you plan to teach will also influence your choices. Theoretical issues can more easily be demonstrated with graphic symbols than with photographs; in teaching a theory, you may choose to use progressively disclosed graphics with verbal labels, so that the learner has time to grasp each new element a bit at a time.

The **medium** you use will also affect the choice of kind and degree of visualization. Human fine motor skills, for instance, are best presented in live-action video or animation; three-dimensional objects, on the other hand, are best depicted as models or holograms, while realistic details are best shown with photography.

The availability of **time and resources** will also influence your choice of kind and degree. Time and resources are practical constraints: How much design and production time can you allocate to this project?

Planning is as time-consuming as production in most development projects. Also consider how much money to allot to this effort. Will these visuals have a short shelf life, or will they be used many times? These considerations will help you decide what kinds of visuals to develop.

Your own **ability to think visually** will also have a significant impact on your planning. You would probably not use a concept-related graphics if you had never done so in the past. However, if you consider nothing but Type I reader frames, you are inhibiting your natural ability to visualize. You will be given an opportunity to enhance your visualizing skills in Chapter 3: Visual Thinking.

Of all the factors that influence the choice of kind and degree of visualization to employ, your ability to think in visual terms will be most persuasive. When you know how to do something that will markedly improve your performance, you will tend to continue doing it. As you increase your ability to visually con-ceptualize what has to be taught, you will grow more competent and confident as a course developer or instructor.

In the educational environment, the course developer (who is often also the instructor) must decide what the learner should see, hear, read, touch, manipulate, or practice in order to learn. The developer determines whether visuals are required and how the graphic artist will render them.

The graphic artist should not decide what the learner should be seeing. The graphic artist can make the screen look good, but it is the course developer who must decide what the learner should see. The course developer can doodle or thumbnail sketch an idea, and graphic artists can turn that same doodle into an elegant visual for use in the classroom. The clearer the thumbnail sketch (also called a rough sketch) and instructions to the artist, the better the product. Similarly, the better the idea, the better the product.

Alternative Solutions to Exercises in Chapter 2

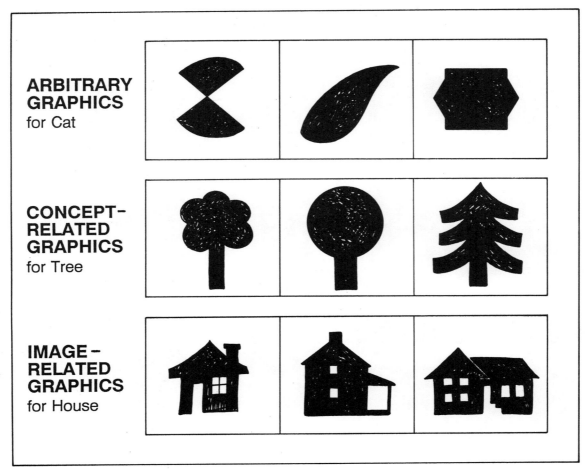

ARBITRARY GRAPHICS
for Cat

CONCEPT-RELATED GRAPHICS
for Tree

IMAGE-RELATED GRAPHICS
for House

Possible solutions to EXERCISE I

Your designs should be compatible with the designs presented in these sample picture series. If they are not, perhaps you should rework your designs. Individual sketching style will make each designer's work look distinct. Your sketching style might be described as detailed, cartoony, primitive, delicate, formal, or realistic. Therefore, your work need not be the *same* as the examples, only *compatible*. Your image-related graphic should read as a silhouette and your concept-related graphic should be a very stylized version of your image-related graphic. (It should represent the essence of the image, minus the details.) Your arbitrary graphic should be an abstract or pure geometric shape. (If your arbitrary graphic looks like the object or thing, then it isn't arbitrary. The image for the arbitrary graphic should be the easiest for you to invent. It may, however, be difficult to make it aesthetically pleasing. An arbitrary graphic's communicative power is closely tied to its pure design qualities.)

photograph	illustration	image-related	concept-related	arbitrary	definition	noun/label

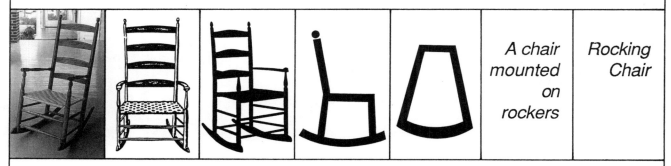

Solution A to EXERCISE II

Solution B to EXERCISE II

Solution C to EXERCISE II

Possible solutions to EXERCISE II

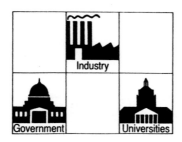

TYPE IV

Verbal/Visual balanced frame

TYPE VII

Pictorial or Graphic symbol frame (pure visual)

TYPE VI

Emphasized graphic symbol frame

AREAS OF MANAGEMENT SUPPORT
- **GUIDANCE**
- **ASSISTANCE**
- **MOTIVATION**
- **ORIENTATION**

TYPE I

Reader frame (pure verbal)

Answers to EXERCISE III

Notes

35

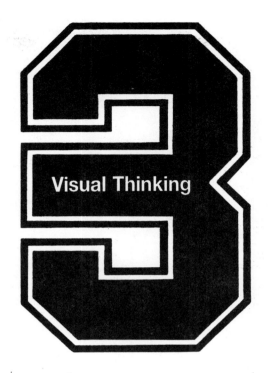

Visual Thinking

Visual thinking is the ability to conceptualize and transform thoughts, ideas, and information of all types into pictures, graphics, or forms that help communicate information. In this section, you will have an opportunity to practice your ability to think visually about:

- Numeric data
- Facts
- Directions
- Processes
- Organizational charts
- Maps
- Chronologies
- Theories
- Attitudes
- Generalizations

You need not be a creative artist to be a visual thinker. Visual images occur naturally as you think. Just mentioning a word triggers a series of images that you can manipulate and control.

An efficient way to conceptualize ideas is to make rough sketches. When given a problem, try to sketch several alternative ways to display the information visually. The exercise of conceptualizing alternatives should contribute to the development of your visual thinking ability.

Note:
As you read this chapter, you will be asked to do some sketching. Please have paper and pen or pencil handy as you read. In most cases, you will be asked to conceptualize verbal information in a visual form.

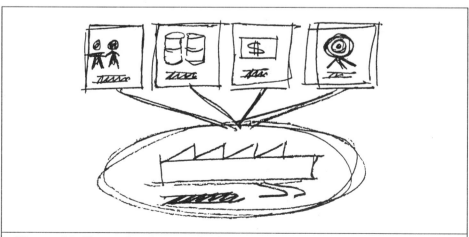

Figure 22. Example of a rough sketch

"Even within a poor society, the poorest are hardest hit. A classification of death rates in Companiganj for 1975 by a Johns Hopkins medical team showed that death rates differed profoundly according to the victim's land-owning status. In Bangladesh, where no land is held, the death rate is 35.8, whereas those who own 3 or more acres have a death rate of 12.2. In between, those with less than 1/2 acre have a death rate of 28.4, while owners of 1/2 acre up to 3 acres have a death rate of 21.5."

A few people can read and understand the data in the paragraph to the left. However, most people need help in organizing this information to see its significance.

There are several ways to organize it – the most common being the table (see Figure 23). At best, this table communicates to a few more people. To most people it remains a bewildering array of data. Numerical data is usually too complex and unfamiliar for most people to understand clearly.

Death Rate in 1975 by Size of Land Holdings (Companiganj, Bangladesh)	
No. of Acres of Land Owned	Death Rate
None	35.8
.01-.49	28.4
.50-2.99	21.5
3.00+	12.2

Figure 23. A table

Perhaps it would be more helpful to present data in the form of a visualization – in this case, a graph. There are several ways to do this. Figures 24 and 25 show two methods for representing the tabular data seen in Figure 23. Each demonstrates boldly and succinctly that as land ownership increases in Bangladesh, the death rate decreases.

This chapter will describe alternative approaches to dealing with numerical data. The goal is to breathe some life into the statistics that are generated in every professional community.

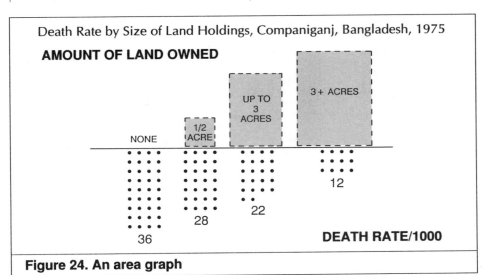

Death Rate by Size of Land Holdings, Companiganj, Bangladesh, 1975

AMOUNT OF LAND OWNED

Figure 24. An area graph

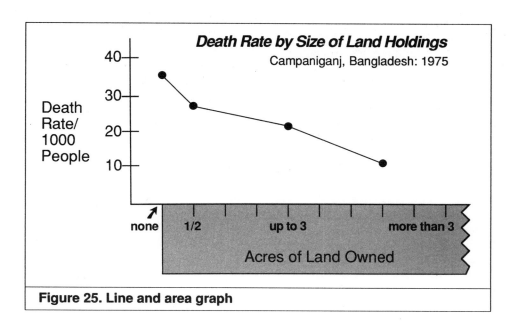

Death Rate by Size of Land Holdings
Campaniganj, Bangladesh: 1975

Death Rate/ 1000 People

40 — 30 — 20 — 10 —

none   1/2   up to 3   more than 3

Acres of Land Owned

Figure 25. Line and area graph

Types of Graphs

The fact that a graph can make a general statement is its greatest strength. A graph should serve to give an impression, indicate a trend or change, or convey a sense of the movement of data. This is usually all an audience needs to know. However, if details or specific facts are needed, they are best retrieved from tables or from prose writing.

Regardless of the medium of presentation – printed handout, computer graphics, slides, overhead transparencies, etc.– there are five well-known graph formats from which to choose:

- Circle graph
- Line graph
- Bar graph
- Pictorial graph
- Map/area graph

These formats are not mutually exclusive; in fact, they are often combined to satisfy specific objectives. Before deciding which graph format is most appropriate for a particular message, it is important to become acquainted with each format and its advantages.

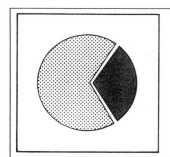 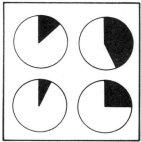 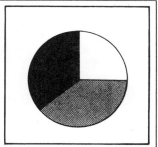

Figure 26. Circle graphs

Hint:
Circle graphs should be used only if each segment or "piece of the pie" is large enough to read. Too many variables make the segments too small and render the graph ineffective in communicating data to an audience.

Circle Graph

The circle graph, often called a pie chart, is an appropriate format to use when the numerical data are to be stated as percentages of a total or a whole (see Figure 26). For instance, circle graphs are useful when information concerns a total age group, all members of a single gender, or total amount of money.

A circle graph is always divided into segments. Simple line patterns, tones of gray, or colors can be applied to these individual segments to create visual contrast. This highlights the relationships between segments; it also compares each segment to the whole. If necessary, more than one circle can be used in a visualization.

Figure 27 incorporates two ideas using circle graphs. It shows (1) the percentage of men versus the percentage of women and (2) the proportional increase in the size of the total populations over time (shown by the change in size of the circles).

Line Graph

The line graph is a useful technique for displaying the overall movement of numerical data over a period of time (see Figure 28). This format can be used to present large amounts of data in a single display; for instance, the flow of events over centuries can be visualized with as much clarity as events occurring within the past year.

The line graph is a format that can demonstrate the highs and lows, the rapid or slow movements, or the relative stability of statistics. In addition, the line graph is an excellent format to use when you need to show comparisons and relationships. Line graphs can incorporate two,

three, four, or more scales to compare the same item in different time periods.

Figure 29 uses the line graph format to show the rise of per capita disposable personal income of Americans from 1970 to 1985. First, the viewer's eye is drawn to read the bold black scale; the viewer then incorporates a second scale (dotted line) that communicates a more complete and accurate economic story. The message of the graph now becomes clear: Although per capita disposable income is rising, it is rising in line with general inflationary prices.

In Figure 29 (a) includes the same data as (b); however, the visual emphasis is reversed. This change in emphasis may come as a result of reevaluating audience needs and/or reconsidering the primary objective of the visual.

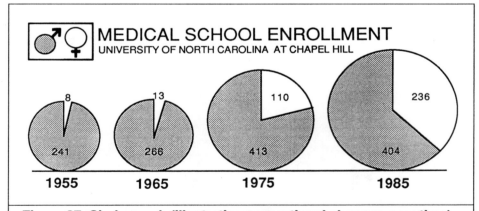

Figure 27. Circle graph (illustrating proportional changes over time)

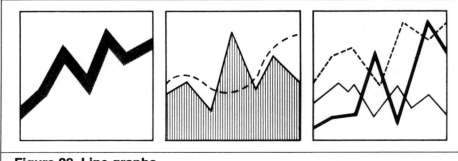

Figure 28. Line graphs

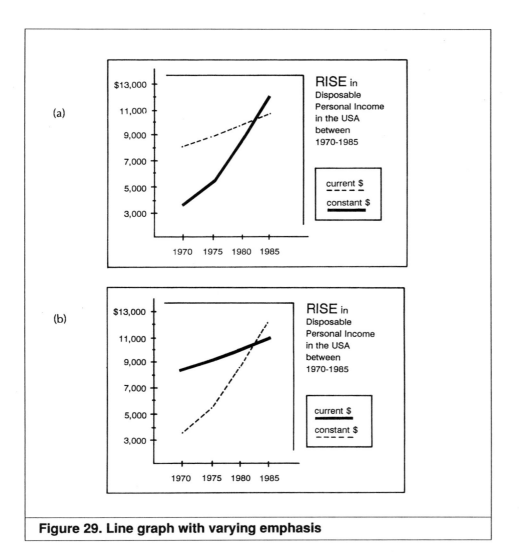

Figure 29. Line graph with varying emphasis

Bar Graph

The bar graph is one of the most convenient and widely used formats for displaying numerical data (see Figure 30). The length of a bar corresponds to the value or amount. When a second bar is added, it is possible to compare data. As more bars are added, more comparisons are possible.

There is a distinction between a horizontal bar graph and a vertical bar graph. The horizontal bar graph usually deals with different items compared during the same period of time. This type of graph is arranged so that items compared are listed on the vertical axis and the quantity or amount scale is on the horizontal axis.

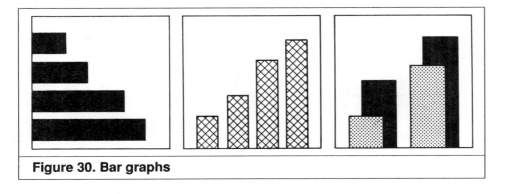

Figure 30. Bar graphs

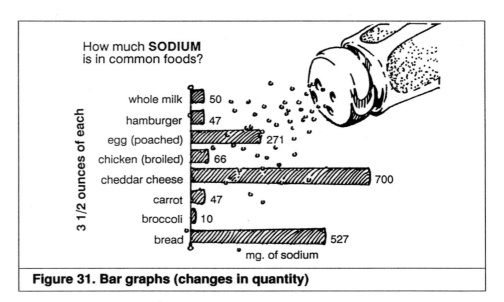

Figure 31. Bar graphs (changes in quantity)

Figure 31 is a horizontal bar graph that focuses on changes in quantities of sodium in various foods.

The vertical bar graph usually deals with similar items compared at different periods of time. The vertical bar graph lists the amount scale on the vertical axis and time or item on the horizontal axis.

Bars can overlap each other to emphasize groupings; they can also use texture or color to dramatize distinctions.

Figure 32 is a vertical bar graph that encourages comparison between two inconsistent items – in this case, the preference of men and women for various sports activities. (The greatest difference is in walking and fishing.)

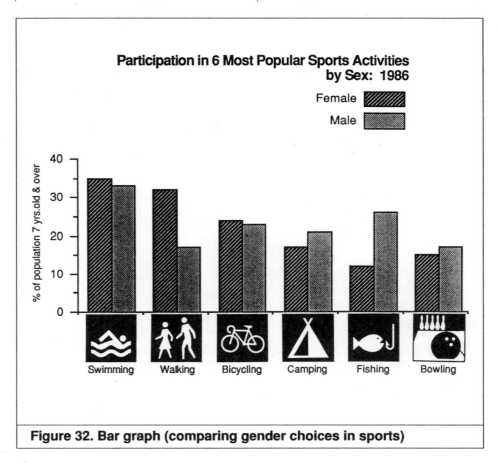

Figure 32. Bar graph (comparing gender choices in sports)

Pictorial Graph

The pictorial graph uses photographs, illustrations, and geometric or abstract shapes to communicate numerical data (see Figure 33). These symbols take the place of conventional circles, bars, and lines.

Pictorial graphs incorporate symbols in two distinct ways. First, a visual symbol can be used as an actual counting unit. Each symbol is given a specific quantitative value and becomes an integral part of the graph; an accurate reading of the graph depends upon the translation of the symbol itself. Figure 34 is an example that uses graphic symbols in place of bars.

Second, a visual symbol can be used as a backdrop for statistical data presented in the more traditional bar or line graph format (Figure 34). Here, symbols are integrated into the graph but are not an essential part of its basic structure. The graph could conceivably be read without the symbol; however, the addition of the symbol strengthens the design and visual interest of the graph.

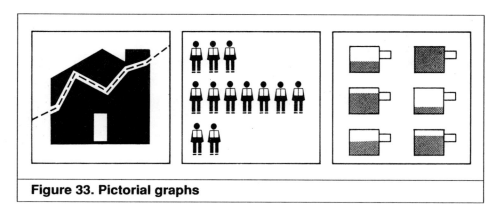

Figure 33. Pictorial graphs

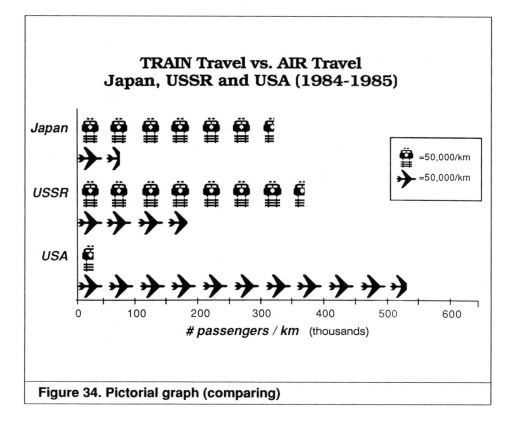

Figure 34. Pictorial graph (comparing)

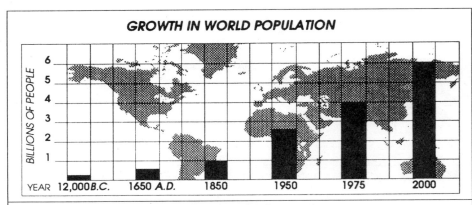

Figure 35. Pictorial graphs (as background)

Hint:
When using photographs for background to present numerical data, take care that the photograph does not obscure the data.

Map or Area Graph

Maps can serve as more than a conventional geographic reference tool; they often provide a versatile and functional way to display numerical data (see Figure 36).

The map sometimes falls into the category of the pictorial graph. If viewed in this sense, the map can be used as a backdrop for data, or as an integral part of the data. In either case, the presence of a map – whether local, state, regional,

  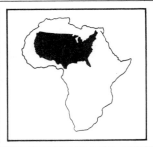

Figure 36. Map/area graphs

GROWTH IN WORLD POPULATION

Figure 37. Map/area graph (frame of reference)

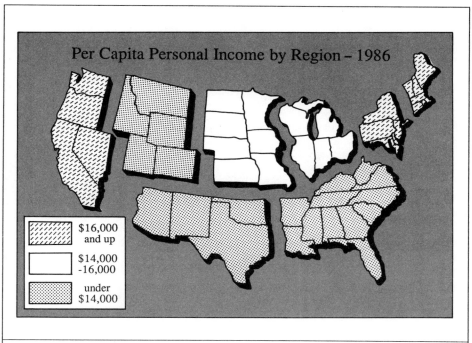

Figure 38. Map/area graph (comparing)

national, or international – gives to the viewer a geographical frame of reference (as in Figure 37).

In Figure 38, the map is used to orient the viewer to the data by states grouped into regions; the shading indicates per capita income in each state. The viewer can quickly see trends as well as the per capita income of each contiguous state.

The area graph (for example, a circle graph) uses either concrete or abstract shapes to divide the whole into its parts. In Figure 39, the area is divided proportionally to indicate how the average dollar is spent.

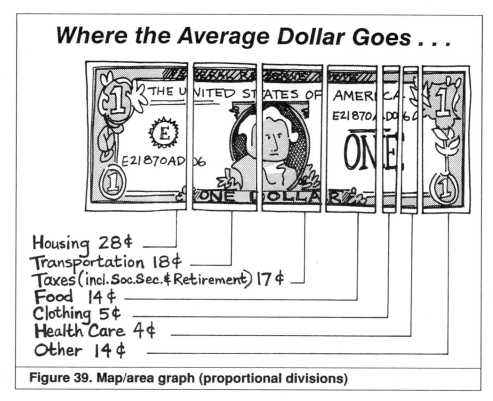

Figure 39. Map/area graph (proportional divisions)

The Titling of Graphs

Regardless of the format, almost every graph has a title or heading. There are basically three approaches to titling. One approach is to use the title to tell the audience the subject of the graph: e.g., "U.S. Birth Rate." The second approach is to tell the audience the major message or point of the graph: "U.S. Birth Rate Declines."

Third, for designers who prefer to have the viewer interpret the major message, a title like "What's Happening to the U.S. Birth Rate?" can draw attention to the message without revealing it. Short, clear, and unambiguous titles encourage viewers to focus quickly on the visual aspects of the graph. Figure 40 illustrates these three approaches to the titling of graphs.

Frequently, more than a title is needed for efficient communication. Information keys, secondary information, and axis labels all require thoughtful planning. Again, use of clear and unambiguous language is your best approach; a heavily labeled graph is often confusing to the viewer.

The following four exercises contain data in tabular form. Each exercise has many possible answers. Solve each problem by applying the various graphing formats discussed above. If your first impulse tells you that the data should be presented in a bar graph format, do a rough sketch using a bar graph. However, be sure to explore other formats such as the area graph or the pictorial graph.

After you have done some rough sketches, look at the possible solutions that appear at the end of this chapter. These alternatives, combined with your own, should prove that there are many ways to communicate even the most elementary data.

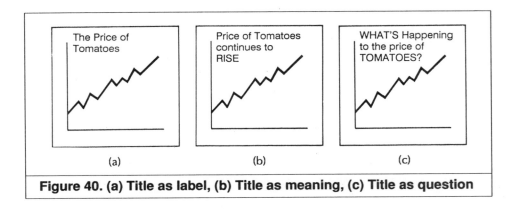

Figure 40. (a) Title as label, (b) Title as meaning, (c) Title as question

Exercise IV

A bit of data

World Travel

Country	No. of Tourists in 1985
Spain	43,235,000
United Kingdom	14,483,000

For every tourist who went to England in 1985, 3 went to Spain.

Rough sketch three alternative ways to present the above data. When your sketches are complete, turn to page 64 to see three possible solutions to this exercise.

Exercise V

Relationships of data

Injuries Resulting from Accidents-USA 1966
(for children over 1 year of age)

Total injuries (years 1-17)	19,000,000
Home injuries	10,000,000
School injuries	3,000,000
Street and highway injuries	2,000,000

The above data represent a fixed place and time (USA 1966) and cover total injuries resulting from accidents. There are several different points of emphasis that could be developed. Graph the above data at least three different ways. When your sketches are complete, turn to the alternative solutions on page 65.

Exercise VI

Progressions of data

Manufacturers' Shipments of Microwave Ovens in the USA

Year	No. of Microwave Ovens Shipped
1982	4,201,000
1983	6,006,000
1984	9,020,000
1985	10,633,000
1986	12,648,000

Rough sketch three different approaches to graphing this data that will visualize the trend in microwave oven shipments from 1982–1986. Then turn to the alternative solutions on page 66.

Exercise VII

Relationships between progressions of data

Urban vs. Rural Percentage of the USA Population 1790-1900

	1790	1830	1870	1910	1950	1990
Urban (%)	5.1	8.8	25.7	45.7	58.8	73.7
Rural (%)	94.9	91.2	74.3	54.3	41.2	26.3

As you sketch three ways to present the data, remember that you are attempting to communicate something about the relationship that exists between these two progressions of data. Look at the three alternative solutions on page 67.

Visualizing Facts, Directions, and Processes

We have all seen visuals designed to teach us facts, directions, and processes. The pull-down map on the wall, the illustrated cookbook, and the laminated emergency directions in the seat pocket of the airplane are all attempts to communicate visually. How well they do this is a direct function of how well they are designed and how well they can be *read*. We must be able to read a visual if we are to understand the message or to act upon it appropriately. Can you read Figure 41?

You are able to understand the meaning of Figure 41 – a pictogram – if you can read the illustrations for "match flame," "wood," "bellows," and "log fire."

You must also have seen bellows before and know how they work. You must also be familiar with the idea that A+B+C=D. Here, the viewer is guided through the message in the traditional left-to-right order of a simple mathematical equation; the plus sign (+) and the equal sign (=) are significant aids to the reading of the message.

Facts

Information about the world, people, places, and things makes up what we call facts. Figure 41 uses illustrations to quickly communicate a fact. Visual cues can also help a learner remember facts. Try your hand at Exercise VIII.

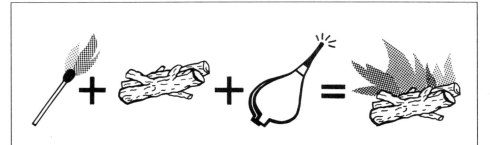

Figure 41. A Pictogram

Exercise VIII
Visualization of a fact

Baby's heartbeats	140 times/min.
10-year-old's heartbeats	90 time/min.
Adult's heartbeats	70-80 times/min.

Sketch a visual that helps the learner understand the change in heartbeats as people age. When you finish, turn to the alternative solutions on page 68 for three possible approaches to this visual.

Hint:
This exercise is related to the first four exercises, which deal with the visualization of data.

Directions

A message is, in essence, a very brief story. In Figure 41, you read the messages in a strictly visual language. As in any good story, the language used was bold, simple, and clear. Furthermore, this visual story employed one of several possible techniques for organizing information, e.g., the use of mathematical symbols. Your attention was actually *directed through* the content by means of the symbols.

The words "directed through" are important here because they imply that what is to be represented has a beginning and an end. It also has an order – a sequence, flow, or movement. Action can be simulated by a series of still images. The point is that when representing directions or processes, it is often appropriate to order information into a sequence, movement, or flow. Aside from mathematical symbols like those used above, you could use arrows or numbers to order information.

Figure 42 indicates how an arrow can be used to show movement of information. Note that the viewer follows the arrow in a direction *opposite* the top-to-bottom orientation traditionally used to present a message on a printed page.

Figure 43 uses numbers to move the viewer through sequential information. The viewer reads the numbers in a clockwise direction. Note that the numbers are large and bold, to help the viewer see where the progression starts and ends.

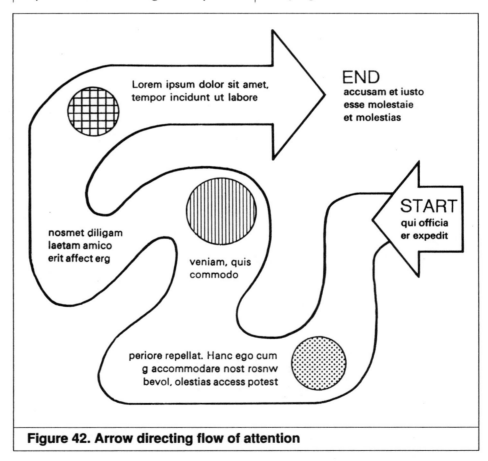

Figure 42. Arrow directing flow of attention

Figure 43. Numbers used to direct flow of attention

Exercise IX

Visualizing a process using arrows and numbers

Prepare a rough design to communicate the process of capturing a scene on film. The important aspect of this exercise is to challenge you to help the viewer see the flow or direction of the steps.

- Observe a scene that you would like to capture on film.

- Load film into your camera.

- Aim camera at the scene.

- Press shutter release to record scene on film.

- Take film to be developed.

- Evaluate finished photograph.

When you finish, refer to the three alternative solutions on page 69.

Often educators have to teach learners how to do something – such as how to wire a circuit or how to use a piece of computer software. At times, instructions for "how to do it" require the learner to perform acts involving motor skills. Visualization can make it easier to learn these skills. Photographs and line drawings are the most common ways to represent instructions.

Many instructions show hands performing the acts of skill. Figures 44 and 45 are photographs of the same event; note that each photo has a different point of view.

Figure 44 is a third-person point of view – that is, the viewer is looking at someone else soldering. Figure 45 is a first-person point of view, and the viewer seems to be doing the soldering. Current theory suggests that the first-person approach is more desirable when teaching people a new set of instructions to follow.

Exercise X gives you practice in visualizing instructions. Incorporate the techniques for demonstrating order and movement in your solutions. Also, maintain a consistent point of view in your visualizations.

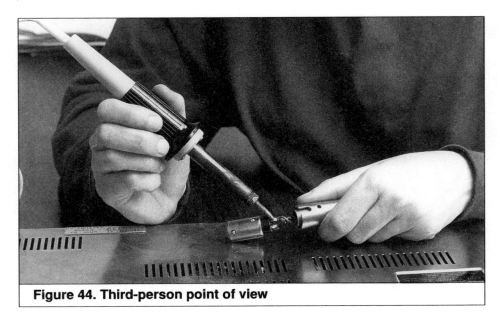

Figure 44. Third-person point of view

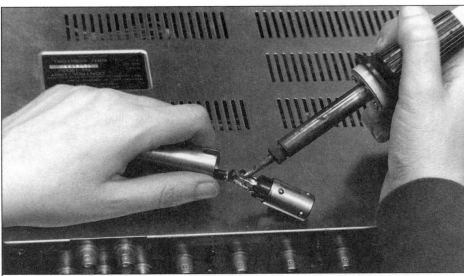

Figure 45. First-person point of view

52

Exercise X

Visualizing instructions

Prepare a rough design for a brochure on how to withdraw cash from an automated teller machine (ATM). Here are the verbal instructions to be visualized:

1. Insert your card into the card reader slot. Be sure the magnetic stripe is facing up.
2. Enter your ID (using the ATM number keys).
3. Press the blue key for CASH WITHDRAWAL.
4. Press the green key to select the account from which you want to withdraw cash.
5. Use the number keys to enter the amount of cash you want to withdraw.
6. Remove your cash, card, and receipt.

When you have finished, check all three alternative solutions on page 70.

Processes

Sometimes we want learners to understand a process without necessarily expecting them to go through the process. We want them to be oriented to the process, have general knowledge about it, or be motivated to take part in the process at a later date. For example, we might want the learner to understand how verbal communication is transferred from New York to California via telephone (an invisible process), or what an insurance claim goes through before payment is made (a visible process). Exercise XI will give you practice in representing process.

The visualizations of facts, directions, and process are necessary if we are to communicate. This section of the guide has started you thinking about alternative ways to make the visualization of facts, directions, and process more stimulating and comprehensible to the viewer.

Exercise XI

Visualizing a process

Prepare a rough design for a wall display that will show how to give blood at the local hospital. The process takes 45 minutes and involves the following steps:

1. Donor gives personal data (medical history).
2. Technician tests for type and health of blood (finger prick).
3. Technician cleans arm.
4. Technician draws blood.
5. Donor rests for 15 minutes.
6. Donor eats snack.
7. Donor resumes normal activities. (No stressful activities for 24 hours.)

When you have finished, check the alternative solutions on page 71 to see three possible approaches.

As a course developer, you will be designing the instruction of broad concepts and large ideas. Some of these concepts are visible (a customer installation plan, for example) and others are more or less invisible (e.g., theories of management). Regardless of how visible or invisible the concepts are, they demand our full talents in order to communicate them effectively.

Visible Concepts

This part of the guide will focus on three kinds of visible concepts: **plans and organizational charts, maps,** and **chronologies.**

Plans and Organizational Charts

Plans are sets of sequences, actions, or goals that are often presented as lists. For example, these are the five steps in a plan to run a campaign for office:
- Establish goals.
- Seek funds and staff.
- Design the campaign.
- Implement the campaign.
- Evaluate the effect of the campaign.

This plan can also be visualized (see Figure 46). The graphic images in each step of the plan help convey the meaning of each step.

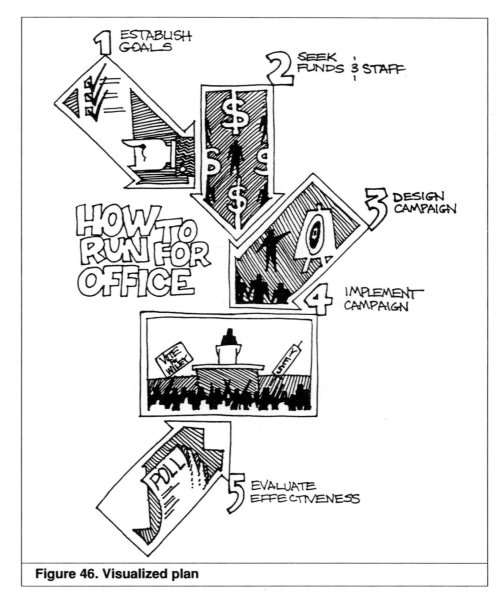

Figure 46. Visualized plan

The Gardener's Schedule for the Year

PLAN	TILL	PLANT	GROW	HARVEST	REST

WINTER	SPRING	SUMMER	FALL

Figure 47. Visualization of a plan in relative time

Figure 47 provides another example of how to communicate graphically the function performed in each step of a plan.

Organizational charts are visual displays of relationships among people in a given setting. Lines and boxes are the cornerstone techniques used to communicate organizational charts. Figure 48 is a classic example of a line-and-staff organizational chart in which the viewer can quickly see line-and-staff relationships.

Though the line-and-staff relationships are clear in Figure 48 the viewer is given no visual cues to meaning, other than the boxes and lines. Figure 49 is an attempt to give the viewer not only line-and-staff relationships but also visual cues to function.

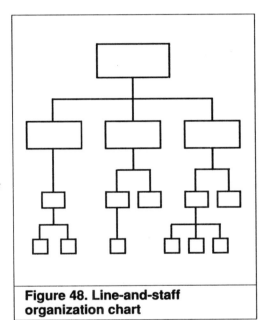

Figure 48. Line-and-staff organization chart

Figure 49. Line and staff and functional relationships

Maps

Maps are one of the oldest visual aids to learning. Scientists have given us a wealth of skills and techniques useful in accurate map-making. This section will deal not with the science of maps, but with the art of maps as visual aids to learning.

What is the purpose of preparing a map? Is it to illustrate the range and quality of a place? To give direction? To illustrate relationships among demographic variables? To simulate the actual place? The purpose or function of the map will dictate its visualization.

Three-dimensional models have great visual appeal. Figure 50 is an example of the use of three-dimensional elements on a map. These maps can be experienced "live," as in the case of table-top models, relief maps, or photographs of three-dimensional models. The use of symbols or models helps orient viewers to key elements or key landmarks.

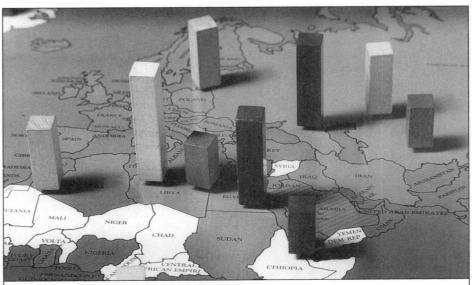

Figure 50. Three-dimensional elements on a map

A map is usually presented in such a way that the different areas of the map are in scale.That is, as you look at Figure 51(a) you can tell that Maine has the largest land area of the six New England states. However, we sometimes want to present a concept or ideas that could distort the map; for example, Figure 51(b) represents graphically the size of the population of each New England state. (For example, Massachusetts is the largest state in terms of population in New England.) Every attempt has been made in Figure 51(b) to retain the overall appearance of each state; only the scale of relative size has been distorted. Now, complete Exercise XIII.

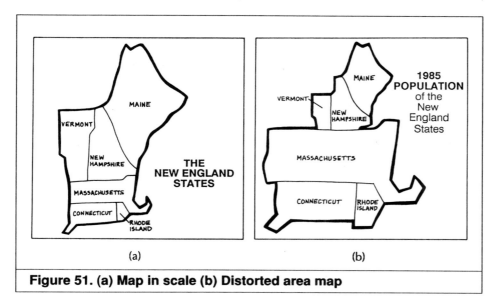

(a)   (b)

Figure 51. (a) Map in scale (b) Distorted area map

Exercise XIII

Visualizing with a map

You want to communicate the three major geographic regions of North Carolina.

1. Coastal plains (elevation range 0 to 300 feet) east
2. Piedmont (elevation range 300 to 1500 feet) central
3. Mountains (elevation range 1500 to 600 feet) west

The following map can be used as a reference:

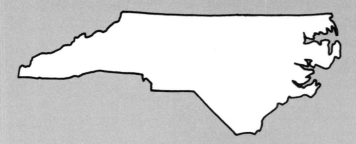

Rough sketch a design for a slide that will communicate this information.

When you have finished, turn to the alternative solutions on page 73 to see three additional approaches.

Chronologies

When dealing with major historic events, periods, or concepts, it is often a challenge to keep events in the proper time perspective. For example, oil is a finite natural resource that was formed over millions of years – yet we are consuming it in only hundreds of years. There are visual solutions that can contribute to our understanding of this relationship.

Figure 52 is a time line that visualizes the amount of time necessary to accomplish each portion of the bread-baking process.

Often we want to communicate the historic evolution of a concept or idea. The time line is a classic example. Figure 53 illustrates the evolution of a ship design. Note that the viewer can see the relatively active and inactive periods of invention.

Figure 52. A time line

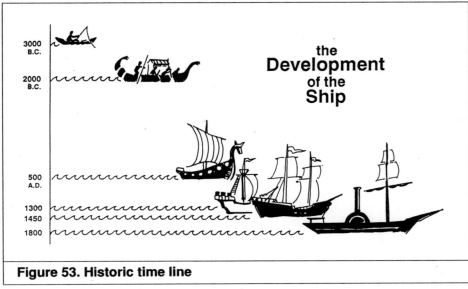

Figure 53. Historic time line

Invisible Concepts

Large ideas often seem difficult to conceptualize in a visual form. The larger the concept – the more complex, the more abstract – the more likely we are to need some type of visualization to present it.

However, the presentation of theories and broad concepts is usually verbal. We talk about ideas; we talk because large ideas usually have no obvious visual counterpart. Yet it seems reasonable to suggest that broad ideas should be visualized as well as verbalized, in order to give the learner at least two sets of stimuli as aids to understanding.

The invisible is the most difficult to communicate. We attempt to explain invisible concepts one way and then another. Explaining something can take us through our complete repertoire of verbal skills: we compare, use analogies, invent mnemonic devices ("Every good boy does fine"), give examples, and so on. However, because the audience has eyes as well as ears, a visualization of the concept may help them begin to understand the concept.

Attempts to visualize the invisible will probably result in new constructs or new ways to conceive ideas. But just as we have a variety of ways to describe verbally, we have a variety of ways to depict visually. We have explored these variations for visible ideas; now the challenge is to work on invisible ideas.

This part of the guide will focus on three kinds of invisible concepts: **generalizations, theories,** and **attitudes.**

Generalizations

Every discipline or field of inquiry produces a set of **generalizations**. Usually, these are the result of much synthesizing of information by experts in that discipline. Sometimes, we want the learner to develop his or her own generalizations; this is a reasonable expectation. But more often than not we want to communicate a generalization to the learner. For example, an anthropology teacher would like the learner to understand the following generalization:

Nomadic, agricultural, and technological societies have different relationships with the environment.

We usually describe concrete examples that lead to such a generalization. Examples include the idea that nomads drink water from ponds, farmers dig wells, and technologists drill wells down into the bedrock (see Figure 54). By studying and discussing the visual, the learner could "discover" the generalization.

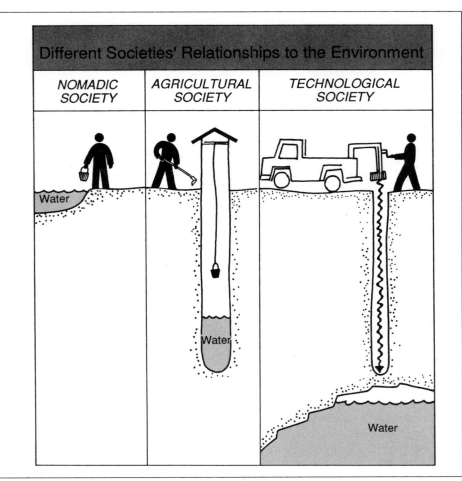

Figure 54. A generalization visualized

Exercise XV

Visualizing a generalization

Design a visual display that would help the learner understand the following generalization: *The investment potential of a nation is primarily influenced by how much money each of its citizens saves in a licensed bank in that nation.*

When you have finished, turn to the alternative solutions on page 75 to see several possible approaches.

Theories

Theories are verified or conjectural formulations about underlying artistic or scientific principles. Einstein's theory of relativity is a classic example of this. Theories abound in all fields; often they are complex, abstract, or "pure." Given these characteristics, it is no wonder that many theories are difficult to comprehend and to visualize.

In trying to explain theories, we often use only words – and neglect the visual possibilities. A judicious combination of words and images could significantly improve the understanding of most theories.

Figure 55 is a visualization of the Shannon-Weaver model of communication. Because it contains visual images combined with verbal cues to meaning, the viewer learns both the essence of the theory and the basic vocabulary for communication in the Shannon-Weaver model.

Theories, models, and abstractions are challenging to visualize because they often demand the invention of new visual configurations. Complete Exercise XVI to practice visualizing invisible concepts.

Figure 55. A theory visualized

Exercise XVI

Visualizing invisible concept

Rough sketch a visual representation of the axiom *The more things change, the more they stay the same.*

When you have finished, turn to the alternative solutions on page 76 to see several possible approaches.

Feelings or Attitudes

Sometimes we want to communicate pure feelings, such as joy, the concept of cooperation, or a sense of loneliness. At other times, we want to communicate processes, data, and theories so that they also include **feelings** or **attitudes**. For example, it is easier to *communicate how* to brush your teeth than it is to *create the desire* to brush your teeth.

We can obviously take photographs with or about feelings, and we can certainly write about feelings. Likewise, we can develop graphic symbols that evoke feelings. Figure 56 is an example of a reader frame that attempts to elicit feelings. Rusty barbed wire should produce strong feelings, because the emotional connotation of barbed wire is stronger than the definition of the abstract term "alienated."

Hint:

Remember to create at least three rough-sketch alternatives before you decide which approach is best. Allow the early stages of conceptualization to be a free-flowing thought process. Once you have several alternatives, you can become more critical in order to establish the best approach.

Conclusion

Visualization can offer a new way to communicate information that we normally only talk about. Whether you are teaching facts, concepts, or processes, visualization will increase the possibility that your educational messages are understood. As you think about the information that needs to be communicated in your classes, seminars, and presentations, make an effort to explore ways to communicate that information in a visual form.

Figure 56. Feeling visualized in a reader frame

Exercise XVII

Visualizing attitudes or feelings

Rough sketch a design for a visual that promotes the attitude to buy American-made products.

When you have finished, turn to the alternative solutions on page 77 to see several possible approaches.

Alternative Solutions to Exercises in Chapter 3

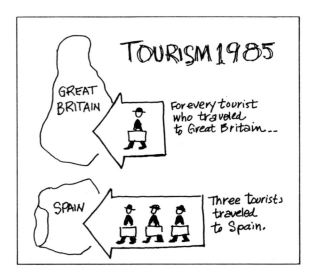

Solution A to Exercise IV

Solution B to Exercise IV

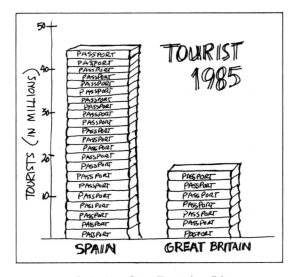

Solution C to Exercise IV

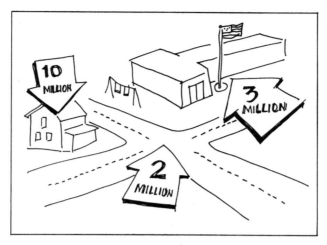

Solution A to Exercise V

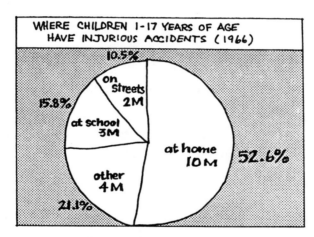

Solution B to Exercise V

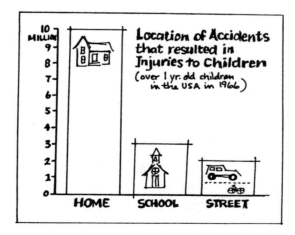

Solution C to Exercise V

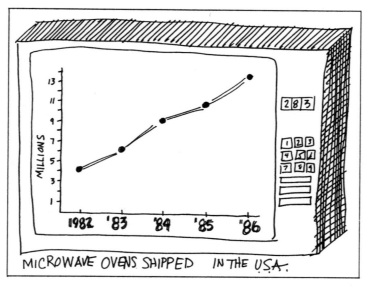

Solution A to Exercise VI

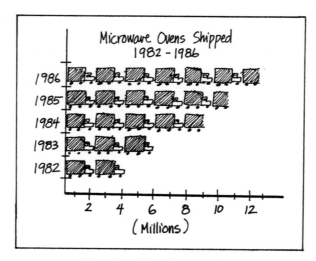

Solution B to Exercise VI

Solution C to Exercise VI

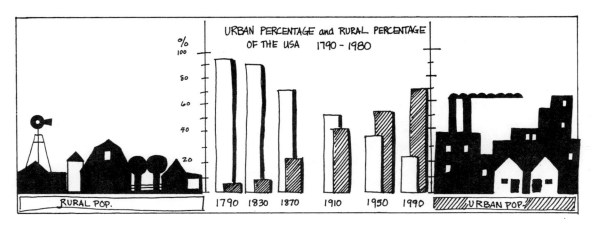

URBAN PERCENTAGE and RURAL PERCENTAGE OF THE USA 1790 - 1980

RURAL POP.

1790 1830 1870 1910 1950 1990

URBAN POP.

Solution A to Exercise VII

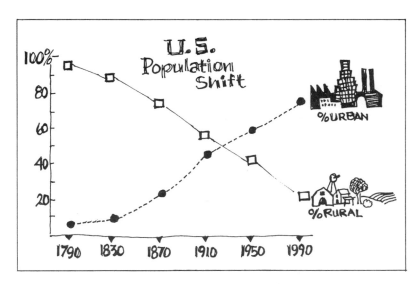

U.S. Population Shift

% URBAN

% RURAL

1790 1830 1870 1910 1950 1990

Solution B to Exercise VII

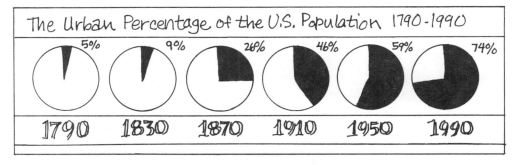

The Urban Percentage of the U.S. Population 1790-1990

5%   9%   26%   46%   59%   74%

1790   1830   1870   1910   1950   1990

Solution C to Exercise VII

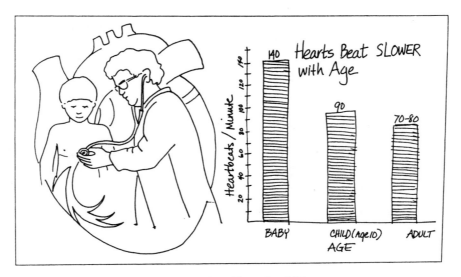

Solution A to Exercise VIII

Solution B to Exercise VIII

Solution C to Exercise VIII

Solution A to Exercise IX

Solution B to Exercise IX

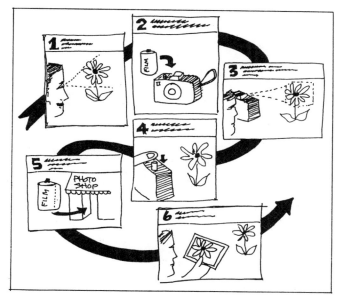

Solution C to Exercise IX

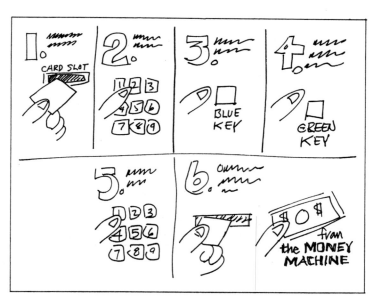

Solution A to Exercise X

Solution B to Exercise X

Solution C to Exercise X

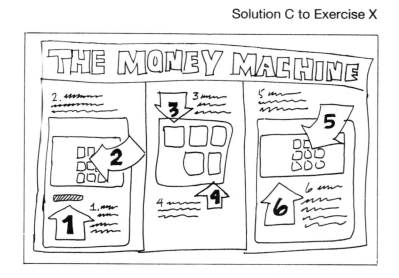

Solution A to Exercise XI

Solution B to Exercise XI

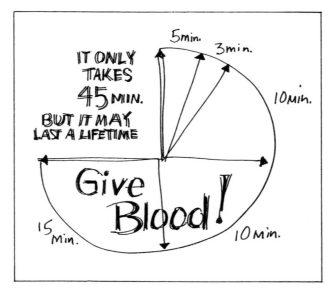

Solution C to Exercise XI

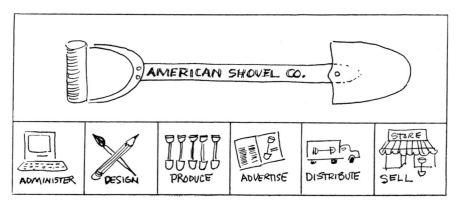

Solution A to Exercise XII

Solution B to Exercise XII

Solution C to Exercise XII

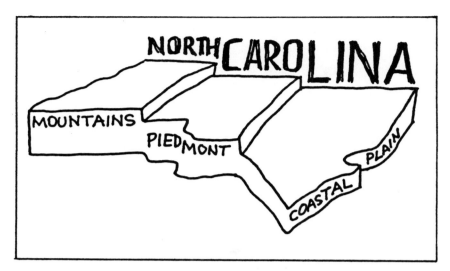

Solution A to Exercise XIII

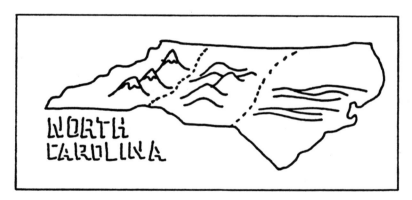

Solution B to Exercise XIII

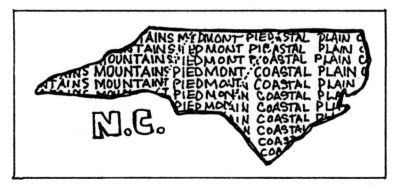

Solution C to Exercise XIII

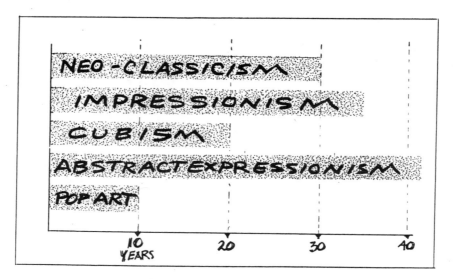

Solution A to Exercise XIV

NEO-CLASSIC
1830-60

IMPRESSIONISM
1875-1910

CUBISM
1900-20

ABSTRACT
1920-60

POP ART
1960-70

Solution B to Exercise XIV

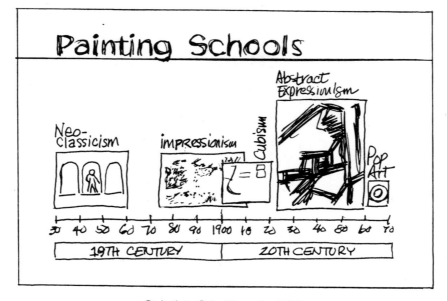

Painting Schools

Neo-Classicism

Impressionism

Cubism

Abstract Expressionism

Pop Art

19TH CENTURY   20TH CENTURY

Solution C to Exercise XIV

Solution A to Exercise XV

Solution B to Exercise XV

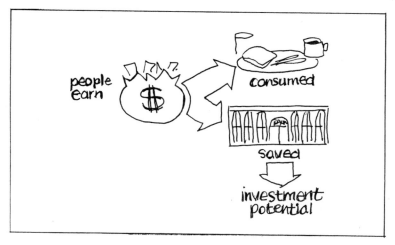

Solution C to Exercise XV

Solution A to Exercise XVI

Solution B to Exercise XVI

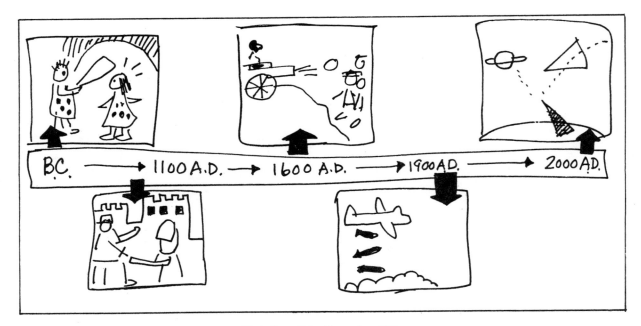

Solution C to Exercise XVI

Solution A to Exercise XVII

Solution B to Exercise XVII

Solution C to Exercise XVII

Visual Design Considerations

Visuals can help you communicate information and ideas. You have already tried your hand at visual thinking by rough sketching visuals to help teach verbal information. These rough sketches can be refined into efficient and effective teaching tools. In order to accomplish your instructional objective, your visuals need to be clear, well composed, and imaginatively conceived and presented.

These three considerations— **clarity, unity,** and **imagination** – are complex and interrelated. This chapter deals with each consideration in detail.

Clarity, unity, and imagination are visual design considerations that course developers and instructional designers can control. When conceptualizing new instructional materials, questions about these three considerations should guide the development of the material. Likewise, the three considerations can be used to judge the worth of existing visuals. They describe the specific steps needed to make your visuals more efficient and effective.

Hint:
The graphic design process is a way of thinking and working. You can increase your graphic awareness by observing graphic design products for inspiration and guidance. Good graphic design, wherever you find it, can improve the visual design of your educational messages.

Clarity

Your visual must be clear, easy to interpret, and to the point. People in your audience must understand what they are looking at on the screen or printed page.

Is the visual clear? The answer is usually a qualified yes or no, because the issue of clarity is comprised of at least seven subquestions.

1. *Are the words and images* **large enough** *to see?*

"How elementary," you may say. How right you are! Surely everyone knows that if you want people to see words and images, those words and images must be large enough for the audience to see. However, in many visual presentations the answer to this simple question would have to be negative.

As you can see in Figure 57, there are many possible combinations of text length and image size.

Words and images, whether you are presenting them on a computer terminal, in a book or handout, or on a projection screen in a classroom, must be large enough to see. The criterion for judging appropriateness of size is directly tied to the situation where the visual is being used. The situation that varies the most is classrooms.

Note:
There are seven questions that can help you make your visuals clear. These questions are on the Clarity rating sheet in the Appendix, page 120. You should have the rating sheet with you as you go through this chapter.

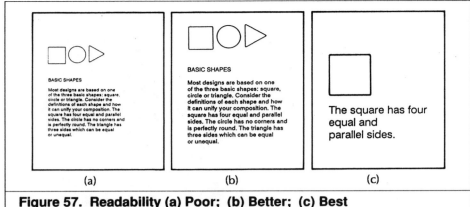

Figure 57. Readability (a) Poor; (b) Better; (c) Best

A good test is to project your visual on a screen. If the image is clear from the farthest point in the room, chances are it will be large enough for all viewers.

The size of the visual is a simple, logical issue–yet it is constantly ignored. The result is unreadable visuals.

2. *Are the words and images* **bold enough** *to see?*

It is the visual weight of letters, illustrations, and graphics that is of concern here. In the world of typography there is a language to describe the weight of letters (see Figure 58).

Illustrations and graphics are often the right size, but rendered in a linestroke that is too light. In Figure 59, note the differences in the following three line drawings of a cat. The cat on the left is almost indescribable from a distance.

Figure 60 illustrates how size and weight are related.

light type

medium type

bold type

extra bold type

Figure 58. Weight of type

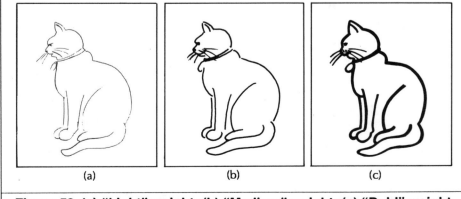

Figure 59. (a) "Light" weight; (b) "Medium" weight; (c) "Bold" weight

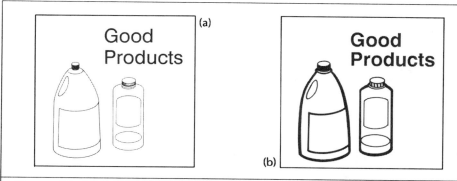

Figure 60. (a) Image large, but not bold; (b) Image large and bold

3. *Is there* **good contrast** *between figure and ground?*

Is there sufficient contrast between the information (words and images) being communicated and the background upon which this information is presented? This is often referred to as "figure/ground relationship." In Figure 61 you see a light ground on the left and a dark ground on the right. Notice the readability of the words and images on these two grounds.

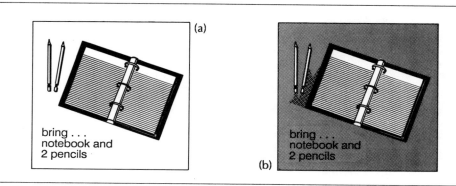

Figure 61. (a) Dark image on light ground; (b) Dark image on dark ground

There should be high contrast between figure and ground. Put another way, light figures read best on dark grounds, while dark figures read best on light grounds. Colors can be seen as light or dark values. You will see this best when you squint at colored presentations – good contrasts are evident even when you squint at them.

When the ground changes in value behind a word or image, this change in value or contrast can reduce the legibility of the word or image. Figure 62 illustrates this phenomenon.

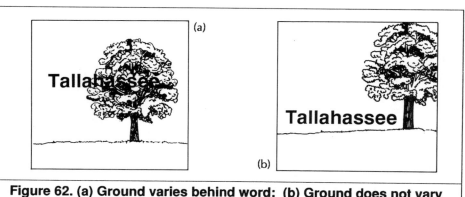

Figure 62. (a) Ground varies behind word; (b) Ground does not vary

Hint:
Early in the creation of your visuals, you should test color, contrast, image and line size, and text font in the delivery environment. You can save significant reworking of visuals by setting standards early.

*4. Is the visual **appropriate** for the intended audience?*

For any visual message to be clear, the visuals themselves must be read, interpreted, and understood by the intended audience. Figure 63 shows some visuals that most people can read, interpret, and understand.

But sometimes we use visuals that may not be understood by everyone. The visuals shown in Figure 64 are less known, extremely specialized, or perhaps easily misinterpreted.

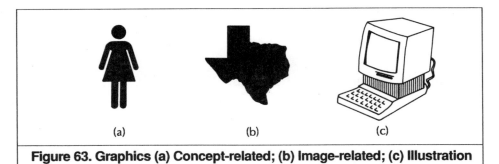

Figure 63. Graphics (a) Concept-related; (b) Image-related; (c) Illustration

Figure 64. (a) Ancient symbol for family; (b) Perennial; (c) Silhouette of Nebraska

Symbols and images from one discipline or culture are not necessarily read as intended by people from another discipline, culture, or age group. Use images that are appropriate for your intended audience. In order to judge whether you are communicating, you should test your approach by asking a sample audience to tell you the meaning of the symbols you use. In any course development process there are formal opportunities to test materials.

*5. What **visual devices** are used to direct the viewer's attention?*

To make a visual clear and understandable, you may do something to the visual that directs the learner's attention. There are many visual devices that you can use, including color, shape, arrangement, texture, line size, and typeface.

When a viewer sees a visual in one of your presentations, he or she begins to interpret it at once. Do not

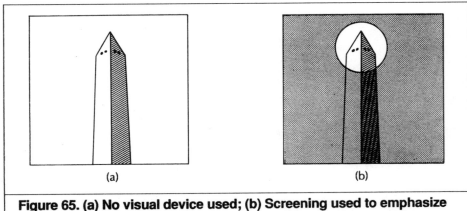

Figure 65. (a) No visual device used; (b) Screening used to emphasize

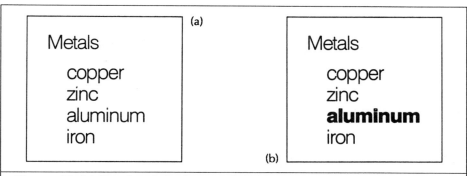

Figure 66. (a) No visual device used; (b) Type weight used to emphasize

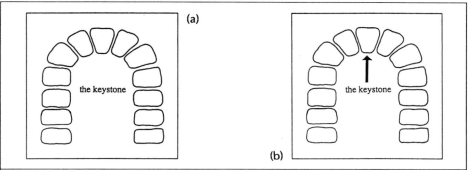

Figure 67. (a) No visual device used; (b) Arrow used to emphasize

expect the viewer to wait for you to explain the visual.

Visual devices that are integrated into the drawing may help the viewer see the focus of your message instantly. Consider using visual devices like those shown in Figures 65, 66, and 67 to guide the viewer's attention.

6. *Does the visual contain only the* **essential information?**

This is an important clarity question. To put it another way, "Is the drawing free of distracting information?"

Many instructors feel compelled to "tell it all" either in words, in pictures, or both. The audience can quickly become overburdened when instructors try to crowd everything into their visuals. Instructors may think they are teaching a lot of material; in fact, they are only confusing and bewildering the audience.

Notice the difference in clarity between (a) and (b) in Figure 68.

Hint:
Put only the essential information in your visuals. If necessary, put details in your handouts.

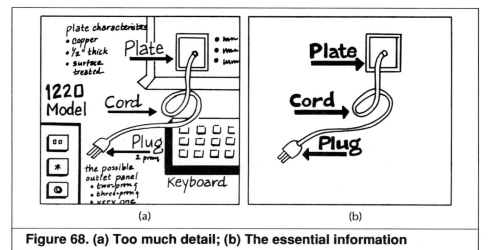

Figure 68. (a) Too much detail; (b) The essential information

A good rule of thumb is to have only *one concept or idea per visual.* Don't try to crowd several concepts or ideas into one visual. This will surely make learning difficult.

When the subject is technical, the information being communicated is frequently quite involved, complex, and detail-oriented. The visuals will tend to be involved, complex, and detailed. This can become a frustrating problem. How do you communicate complex ideas in a *simple* visual way? This problem can be answered in part by our last clarity question.

7. Are appropriate visual **sequencing techniques** *used to present complex ideas?*

There are many ways to sequence information, notably:

- Progressive disclosure
- Establishing and then zooming in
- Panning or tilting
- Simple animation

The following sections show examples of these techniques.

Progressive disclosure

In progressive disclosure, words and/or images appear sequentially as the visual is built up bit by bit. Use this technique to present one element of the concept at a time to the viewer (see Figure 69).

This technique not only addresses the need to break complex ideas into digestible chunks, but also can be used to control an audience's natural tendency to "read ahead" on visuals. Progressive disclosure can be a powerful tool when it is important that the audience understand each part of a concept before addressing the next.

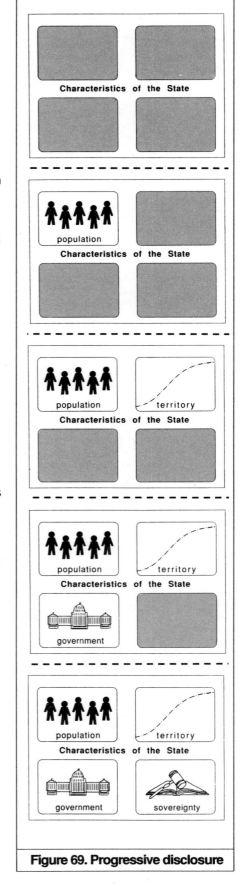

Figure 69. Progressive disclosure

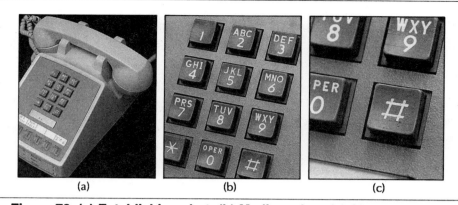

Figure 70. (a) Establishing shot; (b) Medium shot; (c) Close-up shot

Establishing and zooming in on the subject

An establishing shot orients the viewer to the overall subject. For example, say the viewer is learning about the pound key (#) on a push-button telephone (see Figure 70). Starting the lesson with a close-up of the pound key might confuse the viewer. Instead, start with a wider view (establishing shot) of a telephone, then zoom in on the pound key–either video, or a series of photographs or illustrations that show closer views of the telephone until the pound key image fills the screen.

Three to five shots should be sufficient to "establish" where the viewer is to start (the telephone) and where the viewer is to focus (the pound key). When the object is not that well known, you may want to indicate scale by including something that is familiar to the viewer. A human hand is a simple and appropriate indicator of scale.

Panning or tilting

These are film/video terms that describe the motion of a camera. This motion can affect how words and images are presented on a screen. Generally, "panning" is a horizontal movement, as shown in Figure 71(a). Sometimes, educational messages can be best presented by having them move horizontally across the screen. How this is actually accomplished is not the concern here. As a visual thinker you need to decide if the information should move horizontally across the screen. The graphics designers and videographers will work on the best way to accomplish the action.

Tilting is, as you might have guessed, the vertical movement of a camera, as shown in Figure 71(b). The motion of the words and images is very much like "scrolling" on a computer screen.

(a)

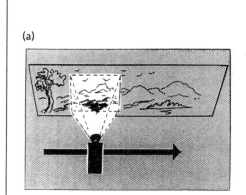

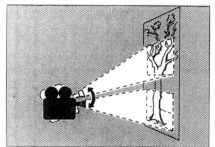

(b)

Figure 71. (a) Panning left to right; (b) Tilting up and down

Simple animation

Animation can be a wonderful way to bring life to still images or to give the illusion of movement. By displaying a series of images, each with a slight progressive change, you can bring movement and activity to the screen.

Animation is traditionally related to cartoon and motion pictures. However, current technologies permit simple animation without having to use complex film techniques. For example, you can animate the flow of data through a computer, or you can show the motion of gears in an assembly. Like other sequencing techniques, animation requires some creative planning and rendering (see Figure 72). As course developers and instructional designers, you will have to plan the animation and work closely with the rendering staff to ensure that key learning points are emphasized.

Summing Up: Clarity

In review, here are the seven *clarity* questions that help you make your visuals clear.

1. Are the words and images *large enough* to see?
2. Are the words and images *bold enough* to see?
3. Is there *good contrast* between figure and ground?
4. Is the visual *appropriate* for the intended audience?
5. What *visual devices* are used to direct the viewer's attention?
6. Does the visual contain only the *essential information*?
7. Are appropriate visual *sequencing techniques* used to present complex ideas?

Use these questions to direct your planning of visuals. Also use them to help guide your critique of existing visuals. Based on the 1 to 5 scale on the rating sheet, your visuals should earn a total score of 35 (seven questions with five "Yes" answers). Anything less should give you the rationale for improving the planning and/or the rendering of your work.

Hint:
*Using the Clarity rating sheet in the Appendix to review **all** of your visuals could be extremely time-consuming. You should use the rating sheet on most of your visuals until you feel comfortable with the ideas embodied in the clarity questions. Thereafter, use the rating sheets only to spot-check your work.*

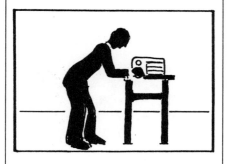

Figure 72. Frames of animation

Exercise XVIII
Evaluating Visual Clarity

Critique figures 73 and 74 in terms of the clarity questions. (Each of the visuals has a major clarity flaw.) Decide which clarity question is primary. When you finish, refer to the revisions described on page 100.

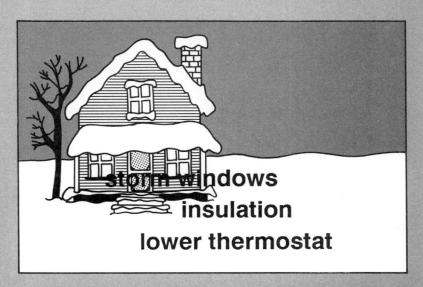

Figure 73. Visual with a clarity flaw (home heating)

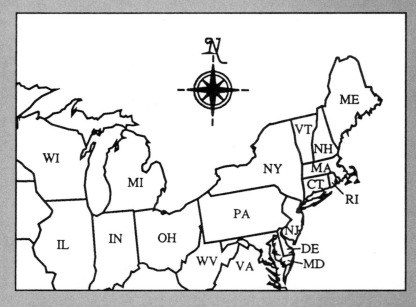

Figure 74. Visual with a clarity flaw (New England States)

Unity is the visual design consideration that focuses on the composition of the visual. The information on the screen may be clear, but it also must be organized in such a way that it facilitates understanding. In other words, it must be well composed. Unity questions have to do with the "look" of the screen.

1. *Are the visual elements (words, pictures, graphic design elements)* **well laid out?**

This is the basic unity question. Layout is a complex and sophisticated subject. Layout, or "composition" as it is known in the fine arts world, is the dimension of visual communication that helps the viewer see words, pictures, and other graphic design elements in an organized relationship. Good layout can facilitate communication.

There are many ways to lay out your visuals. These methods can be classified as either "formal," "informal," or "dynamic" (see Figure 75).

Note:

There are six questions that can help you make your visuals well composed. These questions are on the Unity rating sheet in the Appendix, page 121. You should have the rating sheet with you as you go through this chapter.

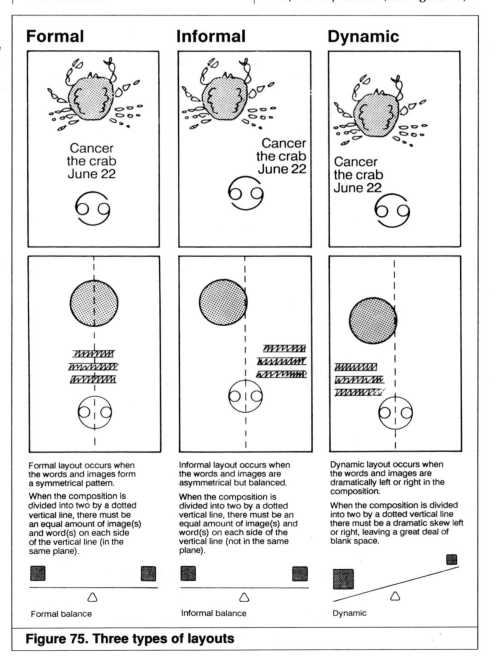

Formal layout occurs when the words and images form a symmetrical pattern.

When the composition is divided into two by a dotted vertical line, there must be an equal amount of image(s) and word(s) on each side of the vertical line (in the same plane).

Informal layout occurs when the words and images are asymmetrical but balanced.

When the composition is divided into two by a dotted vertical line, there must be an equal amount of image(s) and word(s) on each side of the vertical line (not in the same plane).

Dynamic layout occurs when the words and images are dramatically left or right in the composition.

When the composition is divided into two by a dotted vertical line there must be a dramatic skew left or right, leaving a great deal of blank space.

Formal balance

Informal balance

Dynamic

Figure 75. Three types of layouts

A very valuable tool for use in layout is the grid. Grid paper has been used by designers for years. The grid has since moved to the computer and has evolved as a valuable tool in publishing. As a visual thinker you will be making layout suggestions when you present your rough sketches to a graphic artist for rendering. The grid can be used to help lay out your ideas.

Figure 76 is a grid. Use it behind tracing paper, sketchpad paper, or regular white drawing paper. In the following example, you can see how a grid is used to plan, rough sketch, and execute a well-designed layout. Note how the grid is used to direct the layout. Even the visual without the grid gives the viewer very strong clues that a grid was used.

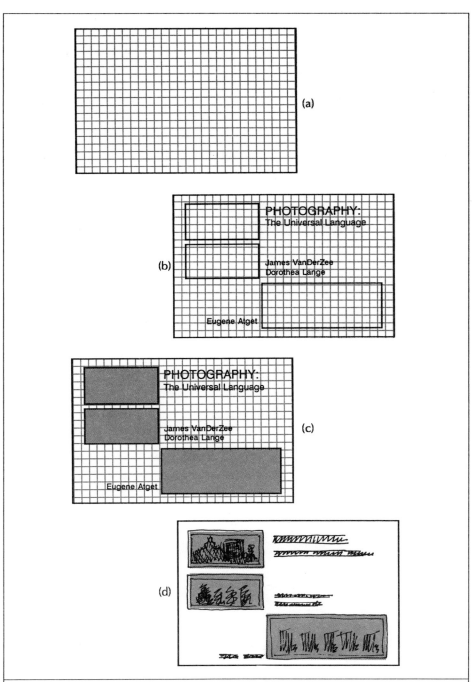

Figure 76. (a) A grid; (b) Sketch over grid; (c) Finished art on a grid; (d) Finished product

Hint:
Browse through magazines, newspapers, and other print material to see how pictures and text are laid out. Study layouts that catch your eye and appeal to you. What is it about these layouts you could use in your visual design?

How information is laid out (formally, informally, or dynamically) is a very important visual consideration. Layout is, of course, secondary to your instructional objectives and the information to be presented in your visual. Decide what words, illustrations, and graphic symbols are needed, then start moving them around on your sketchpad. The layout will emerge from the manipulation of these elements.

If layout design does not come easily to you, or if the elements of a good or poor layout are not evident to you, do not feel inadequate to the task. Clearly, layout is a skill area that takes years of practice; in fact, many course developers find the process to be mystifying and best left to the graphic artist, who is already well versed in the skills of composition. Part of the problem for the novice layout sketcher is the difficult notion that you not only decide

what words and pictures are to be seen, but also what blank space will be seen. *It is this blank space that often dictates the effectiveness of the layout.*

2. *Does the* **margin** *unify or add to the composition of the visual?*

The concept of "margin," "border," "frame," or "mat" describes the space around the edge of your visual message. It's a "fence" that keeps words and images in the corral. In most visual presentations the margin helps the viewer focus on the concepts or words, because the concepts reside inside the margin. Figure 77 shows examples. Margins are not always necessary or even advisable. Clearly there are times when words or images should even "bleed" off the screen. See Figure 78 for an example.

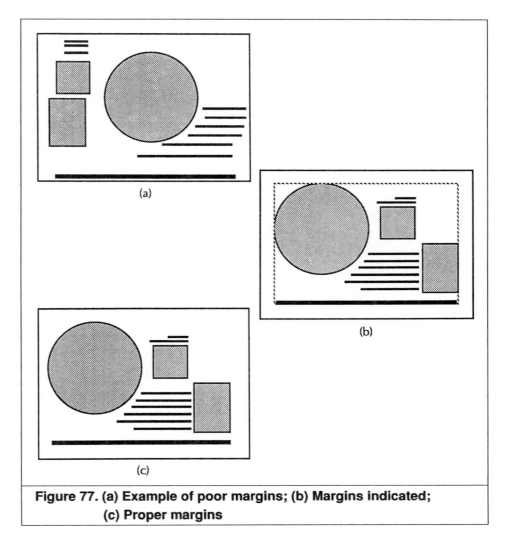

Figure 77. (a) Example of poor margins; (b) Margins indicated; (c) Proper margins

the
power
tool
of yesteryear

Figure 78. Illustration of "bleeding" off the bottom of the frame

3. *Does the entire message (words and images)* **fill the screen?**

You need to fill the screen in order to make an effective composition. The composition itself should be what the viewer sees. Novice, and sometimes experienced, instructors design visuals that look more like a presentation of background than a presentation of words and images. Figure 79 shows examples of compositions that have (a) too much background and (b) the appropriate amount of background.

Hint:
A good rule of thumb is to be "big, bold, and graphic." Zoom in close to images and objects, but remember to leave an appropriate margin.

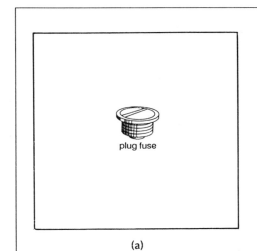

plug fuse

(a)

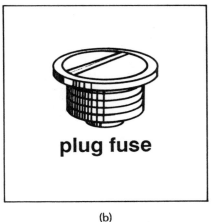

plug fuse

(b)

Figure 79. (a) Good layout, but doesn't fill screen;
(b) Good layout that does fill the screen

Hint:

As a course developer, instructor, or subject matter expert, you may think everyone knows everything that is being presented and that labels are incidental. This is not the case. You should make all labeling clear in the visual or in your verbal presentation of the visual.

Hint:

To make the composition direct the viewer's attention to what counts, you may often have to resort to very dramatic angles or points of view. Good composition of "live" shots requires careful planning and execution. Often the conventional visual point of view is not the best angle for photography. Tell your photographer your instructional intent so that the visuals have the appropriate viewing angle.

4. *If words are used, is it clear* **which words go with what pictures?**

This seems to go without saying, yet there are many visuals in which it is quite evident that verbal labels do not clearly relate to their visual counterparts. Figure 80 shows examples of (a) confusing, and (b) clear placement of verbal labels.

5. *Does the composition direct the viewer to the* **center of attention?**

Often "live" shots or illustrations are only tangentially related to the message or concept that is to be communicated. Instructors frequently rely on narration to direct the viewers' attention. However, you can use composition to direct atten-

tion to the main event. For example, if you want to illustrate the proper procedure for hand-washing, you should use the angle (perspective) shown in Figure 81(b) because it shows the action, while Figure 81(a) merely alludes to the action.

6. *Does the composition* **support what is being taught?**

Composition can serve a purpose other than making the presentation look good. For example, if the objective is to teach the learner that Process A involves five steps, which then start all over again, then Figure 82 (b) is an example of how the composition/layout contributes to the instructional objective.

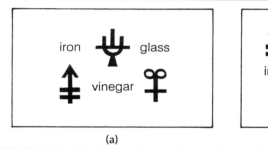 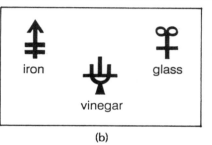

(a)   (b)

Figure 80. (a) Confusing placement of labels; (b) Clearly placed labels

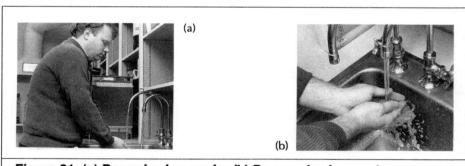

Figure 81. (a) Poor viewing angle; (b) Proper viewing angle

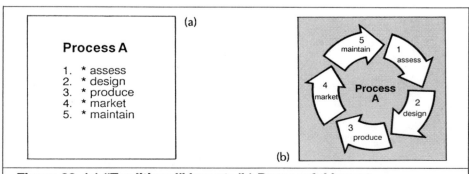

Figure 82. (a) "Traditional" layout; (b) Purposeful layout

For review, here are the six *unity* questions that help you make your visuals clear:

1. Are the visual elements (words, pictures, graphic design elements) *well laid out?*

2. Does the *margin* unify or add to the composition of the visual?

3. Does the entire message (words and images) *fill the screen?*

4. If words are used, is it clear *which words go with what pictures?*

5. Does the composition direct the viewer to the *center of attention?*

6. Does the composition *support what is being taught?*

Use these questions to direct your planning of visuals. Also use them to help guide your critique of existing visuals. Based on the 1 to 5 rating scale on the rating sheet, your visuals should earn a score of 30 (six questions with five "Yes" answers). Anything less should give you the rationale for improving the planning and/or the rendering of your work.

Exercise XIX
Evaluating Visual Unity

Critique Figures 83 and 84 and in terms of the unity questions. (Each of the visuals has a major unity flaw.) Decide which unity question is primary. When you finish, refer to the revisions described on page 101.

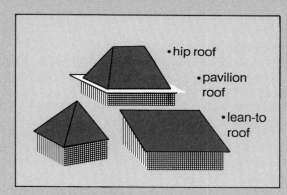

Figure 83. Visual with unity flaw (roof types)

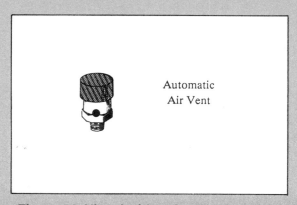

Figure 84. Visual with unity flaw (air vent)

Hint:
*Using the Unity rating sheet in the Appendix to check **all** of your visuals could be extremely time-consuming. You should use the rating sheet on most of your visuals until you feel comfortable with the ideas embodied in the unity questions. Thereafter, use the rating sheets only to spot-check your work.*

Note:
There are five questions that can help you make your visuals more compelling. These questions are on the Imagination rating sheet in the Appendix, page 122. You should have the rating sheet with you as you proceed through this chapter.

The third major visual design consideration has to do with making visuals compelling, interesting, and memorable. Learners are going to learn and remember more when the instruction is compelling. Visuals can contribute a little or a great deal to your instruction. Make sure that your visuals help carry the load; make the visuals work for you in a substantial way.

·In many respects imagination is the most difficult of the visual design considerations. A visual can be clear and well composed, yet boring. Even more disheartening, the visual can be clear and well composed, yet can be assigned little or no role in communicating the information. A complete set of bold reader frames, one after the other, may be well composed and predictable, and may be difficult to fault. However, these visuals may not hold the viewer's attention. It is thus fair to ask what role they play in helping the viewer understand and remember what is being taught.

On the other hand, some visuals may be very imaginative, but not relevant to your instructional objective.

1. *Does the visual "connect" to* **the learner's existing knowledge** *and interest?*

It is very important to make connections between what the learner already knows or cares about and what you want to convey. Visuals can help make these connections. However, for you to make meaningful use of this idea, you may have to do some research related to learner interests and the module that you are teaching. When you use objects and actions familiar to your learner, learning is facilitated.

For example, assume that you are a geometry instructor. You have learned that your new class of learners is very interested in ancient history, particularly the Greeks and the Romans. Therefore, start your lesson with some pictures of structures from ancient history (Figure 85a). Then, show a geometric drawing of the Greek formula for creating a pleasing rectangle (called the "golden section") (Figure 85b); then tie the ancient structures to the geometry you want to teach (Figure 85c). In this example you began with student interests and then moved to your instructional objective. This technique is very effective.

Motivation is a key factor in getting your message across. You need to make the links between what you are teaching and what makes your learners sit up and take notice.

Not only do you need to acknowledge the learner's knowledge and interest, but also you need to acknowledge the precise situation in which the learner is starting the lesson. The situation includes the room in which the learning is taking place, the learner's feelings about this experience, who's sitting next to him or her, the time of day, current season of the year, degree of familiarity with the town or place where this instruction takes place, and so on. When a presentation starts with this kind of acknowledgment, the learner often feels that the instructor is very aware of the student's feelings at that precise moment.

Hint:
The audience analysis conducted for your course should include questions that help you establish student preferences and background.

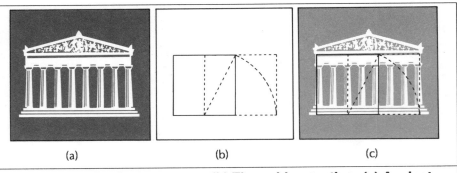

(a)   (b)   (c)

Figure 85. (a) Ancient structure; (b) The golden section; (c) Ancient use of the golden section

2. *Does the visual have a **style that relates to** the other visuals being used in this lesson?*

From across a crowded room you can recognize the difference between *USA TODAY* and *The Wall Street Journal*. Even from that long distance, it is principally the visual style of each that tells you which is which. You see the difference: color, graphic, layout, typeface, and many other visual factors contribute to your seeing a style or lack of style in a visual.

Within each of your lessons or presentations, you can enhance retention and interest by using a visual style that sets your lesson apart from others. Continuity of style (such as the consistent use of graphic images, font, color, size, layout, etc.) helps your audience orient themselves within a presentation, or in a series of presentations. Figure 86 shows examples of format style.

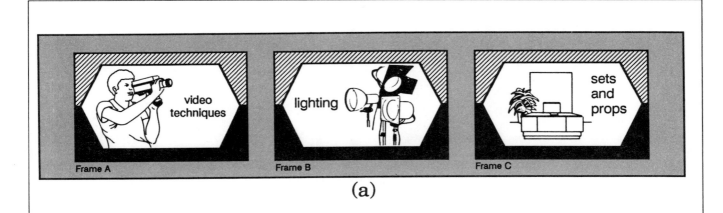

(a)

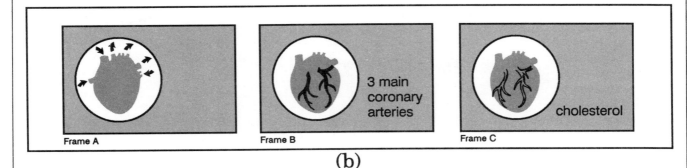

(b)

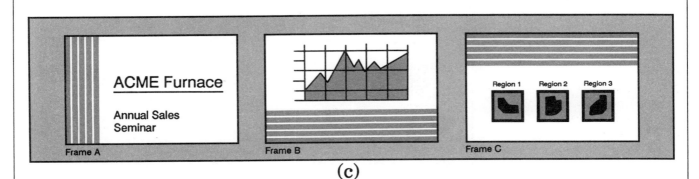

(c)

Figure 86. Examples of consistent format styles

3. *Does the visual **gain the attention** of the viewer?*

You may have trouble answering this question without trying your visuals out on the intended audience. If you don't **gain** the viewer's attention in the first place, then all else is futile. The visuals you use can play a significant role in gaining attention (see Figure 87).

Start with your alternative ways to visually present your concept or idea, then ask how could these ideas be presented in a way that gains attention. Use a visual metaphor or analogy. Also, use color in supportive ways. Use changes in typeface, both in size and kind. Use visuals that are the opposite of what you are saying.

An unexpected title may also gain attention, see Figure 88.

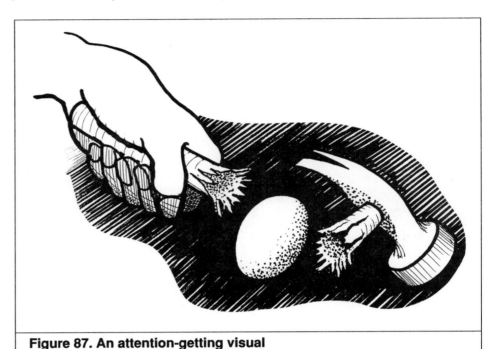

Figure 87. An attention-getting visual

SNOW WHITE and the 2 dwarfs

Figure 88. An unexpected title

4. *Does the visual **hold the interest** of the viewer?*

Not only must you gain the attention of the viewer, but also you must hold the interest of the viewer. A presentation holds the viewer's attention when the rhythm, layout, and pace are not predictable. Once the viewer begins to anticipate what is coming next, he is apt to stop looking or at least pay less attention to the screen. Both gaining attention and holding viewer interest are important considerations. Highly motivated learners have the ability to learn in spite of the instruction. Do not mistake polite attention for true interest.

Holding the viewer's interest requires that you consider not only the visual you are designing or evaluating, but also all the visuals that come before and after it in the presentation. It is no small task to hold the viewer's interest throughout the entire presentation. In testing visuals with the target audience, ask questions designed to measure how well the visuals hold the viewer's interest. Keep this criterion in mind as you periodically evaluate your work.

5. *Does the visual present the information in a way that helps the viewer **remember** the information?*

The ultimate goal of education is to have the learner remember and use the ideas or information presented and discussed in class. Often the learner remembers material that is presented in a unique or intriguing way. Both the words and the visuals work together to facilitate understanding and remembering.

Take a moment now to think about the visuals presented thus far in this guide. Which ones present information you remember? Try to analyze why these visuals were particularly effective.

Summing Up: Imagination

In review, here are the *imagination* questions:

1. Does the visual "connect" to **the learner's existing knowledge** and interest?

2. Does the visual have a **style that relates to** the other visuals being used in this lesson?

3. Does the visual **gain the attention** of the viewer?

4. Does the visual **hold the interest** of the viewer?

5. Does the visual present the information in a way that helps the viewer **remember** the information?

Use these questions to direct your planning of visuals. Also to help guide your critique of existing visuals. Based on the 1 to 5 rating scale on the rating sheet, your visuals should earn a score of 25 (five questions times five "Yes" answers). Anything less should give you the rationale for improving the planning and/or the rendering of your work.

Hint:
Here are some suggestions for holding viewer interest:

1. Vary the kinds of visuals that you use–mix reader frames with illustrations and with photographs. Try not to have several reader frames follow each other in sequence.

2. Use progressive disclosure in random or reverse order, rather than top-to-bottom order.

3. Use color to vary the screens. This can be done in a way that makes color contribute to the learning.

4. Break up screens into areas that suggest a multi-image format.

Conclusion

When you ask the fundamental question "What role does this visual play in the lesson?" you are being reasonable. When the visual has a purpose, it is well on its way to being remembered.

You should attend to all of the questions under each of the visual design considerations. Use the three rating sheets to systematically review your work. Note the 1 to 5 scale on each check sheet. Your goal is to have every visual rated as high as possible. There are seven *clarity* questions, six *unity* questions, and five *imagination* questions. A rating of 5 for each question will give you a grand total of 90, which should be the target score for your visual.

As you use questions in the visual design considerations, you will become increasingly aware of the fact that to adjust or change a visual so as to get a higher rating (ultimately a 5) on one question will affect another question and its rating. The questions are dynamically interrelated.

Note:
To use the rating sheets on every visual in every class presentation would be very time consuming. You should review the rating sheets while designing visuals, and then use them to randomly spot-check your visual plans or your finished products. Some questions cannot be answered without the help of viewers from your intended audience.

Exercise XX
Evaluating Visual Imagination

Critique Figures 89 and 90 in terms of the imagination questions. (Each of the visuals has a major imaginative flaw.) Decide which imagination question addresses the major flaw in each visual. When you finish, refer to the revisions on page 102.

Figure 89. Visual with an imaginative flaw (flower sales)

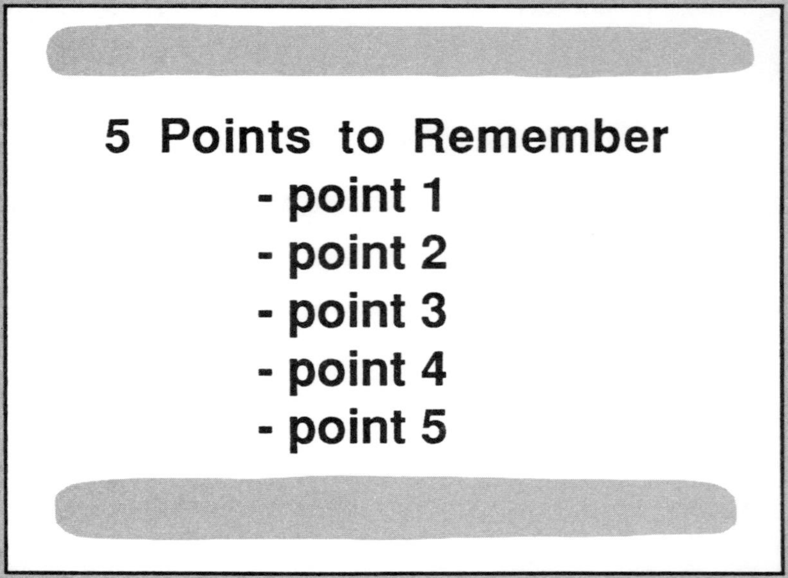

5 Points to Remember
- point 1
- point 2
- point 3
- point 4
- point 5

Figure 90. Visual with an imaginative flaw (remembering 5 points)

Revised Visuals for Clarity, Unity, and Imagination Exercises

Solutions to Exercise XVIII
Evaluating Visual Clarity

In Figure 73, the word "storm" was difficult to read. If you chose question 3, you are on the right track. Figure 91 below is an improvement over the original version. The word "storm" is on a white background, as are the other words.

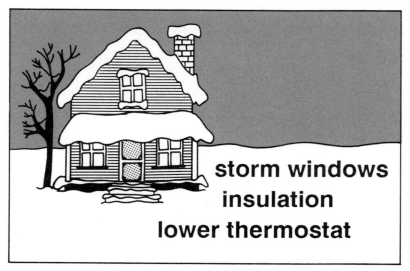

Figure 91 Revision of Figure 73

Figure 74 may be intended to help the learner see the New England states; however, it does not explain which ones they are! If you chose question 5, you are on the right track. Figure 92 helps the viewer quickly locate the New England states, and understand their relationship to the neighboring states of the Northeast.

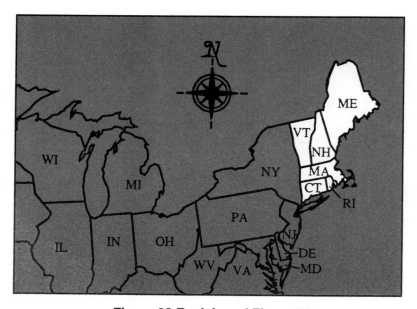

Figure 92 Revision of Figure 74

Solutions to Exercise XIX
Evaluating Visual Unity

Figure 83 needed help. The learner could not tell which words went with which roof type. If you chose question 4, you are on the right track. Figure 93 places the verbal labels in clear relationship to the visual images. In addition, the overall layout is more unified, and the diagonal lines in the upper left and lower right add a bit of style to the presentation.

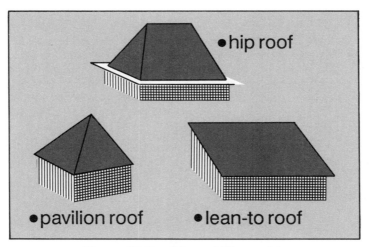

Figure 93 Revision of Figure 83

Figure 84 had too much field and not enough figure. If you chose question 3, you are on the right track. Figure 94 illustrates how the word and image can fill the screen and still leave an appropriate margin around the important elements.

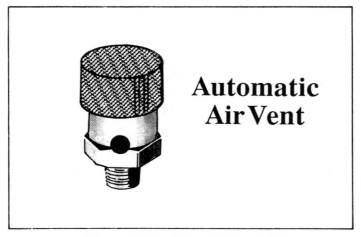

Figure 94 Revision of Figure 84

Solutions to Exercise XX
Evaluating Visual Imagination

In Figure 89 the word "sales" could be more attention-getting. If you chose question 3, you are on the right track. Figure 95 below is a reader frame with visual clues to meaning. Window boxes are the symbol of urban gardening; the "L" in the center of the word "SALES" is in a natural position to become the stem of a flower. What other ideas do you have about revising this visual in an imaginative way?

Figure 95 Revision of Figure 89

In Figure 90 it was hard to remember how many points there are to remember. If you chose question 5, you are on the right track. What devices do we know that help us to remember? A note on the refrigerator door? An acronym? A string around the finger? Why not five strings on five fingers to make it easy to remember the number of points? (See Figure 96.)

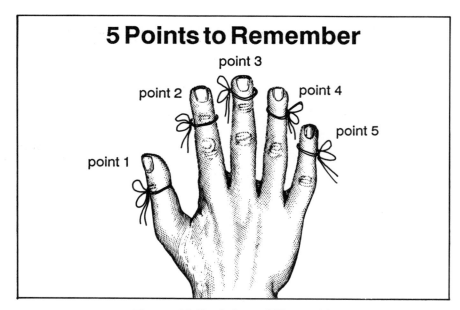

Figure 96 Revision of Figure 90

Notes

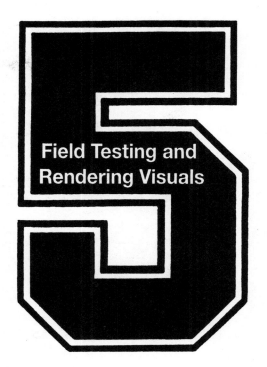

Field Testing and Rendering Visuals

Visual thinking, conceptualizing, and designing have been the major focuses of this guide. Your skills have been tested as you sought alternative approaches to the various EXERCISES. You have been challenged to think in visual terms and rough sketch visual ideas. Often you entertained more than one visual idea or conceptualization. Which one of your many ideas is the best one? Which one is the most instructional? Which is the most attention-getting? Which is the most efficient and effective? Which is the best layout? And once this "best" one has been chosen, how should you convert the thumbnail sketch into a finished product? This chapter focuses on field testing and rendering considerations that will help answer the above questions.

Choosing Your Best Alternative

Two good ideas may be worse than one good idea. That is, it might prove to be quite a dilemma, trying to decide which of two or more good ideas is the one that will communicate the message.

Often you can tell from your own experiences which of your ideas or rough sketches is best. Perhaps an even better way to decide among alternatives is to field test your ideas on your peers and on a sample of your intended audience. Ask a group of your peers to critique your visuals. They will give you feedback on accuracy, appropriateness, and other aspects about which you may have questions. Peer review may lead to suggestions for change. Weigh the suggestions and then follow the suggestions that sharpen the message and contribute

to potential learning. Now you are ready to conduct an intended audience field test.

Select a small sample (six might do) of your intended audience. Arrange to talk to them one at a time. As you begin your interview tell them the purpose of the visuals (e.g., "This visual is intended to help you understand and remember the four parts of a flower."). Next, show your interviewee your sketches in order of preference. Ask him or her to tell you why the alternatives are ranked in that particular order.

This preference testing by a sample of your intended audience can help you decide which alternative to have rendered into final form. However, the fact that the intended audience preferred one sketch over another may not necessarily mean that the preferred sketch will produce the most learning. You can, of course, field test the sketches regarding learning gain. This technique requires some advance planning. The intended audience sample (in this case at least 30 subjects) must be identified. They all must be given a pretest that measures their knowledge of the parts of a flower. They then must be assigned to one of three subgroups. Show one of the alternative sketches to one of the subgroups. (For example, show alternative sketch A to subgroup 1, sketch B to subgroup 2, and sketch C to subgroup 3.) Next give everyone a post-test. The alternative that produces significant learning gain may well be your best example; however, that which is significant may be difficult to discern without using statistical methods.

Sophisticated field testing of alternative ideas through intended audience preference testing and/or assessing learning gain is time consuming. Often, you do not have the time or the resources for such sophisticated research. If you do choose the route of developing a meaningful field test, a word of caution. Be sure that your institution (or client) is committed to giving time to evaluating and using the results to revise the presentation and perhaps repeat the field-testing process. If you are under a mandate to conduct field testing of visual plans, please be advised to seek the advice of an evaluation consultant.

Rendering Your Visual Presentation

Once a thumbnail sketch has been selected, the next task is to render it in a final form. Is it to be a 35mm slide, PC graphic, overhead transparency, handout, job aid, 3-D display, or some other medium? Media format, cost restrictions, and design considerations will influence the way you choose to render the finished product.

Who will actually do the rendering? You may if you have the talent and can afford the time that it takes. Or you can hire someone else to render the conceptual sketches.

If you render the finished product, work from your strengths. That is, if you work well in pen and ink, render your idea in pen and ink techniques. Don't try to work in materials or techniques that are the materials and techniques of someone else! Don't try to imitate others! Be yourself! The results of your work will have much more integrity and personality than if you were to imitate someone else. You might find that you render ideas in one medium better than in another. That is, you may be better at slide production than you are at overhead transparency production. If so, you've found a strength – work on it, sharpen it, get even better.

This is not to say that you should not work on your weaknesses. You should be working at all times to add to your repertoire of skills. You should recognize your strengths, and use them. You should recognize your weaknesses and forego working on them during work hours. Your organization may not find it cost-beneficial having you rendering any visuals.

If you are going to ask someone else to render art work for you, here are some suggestions. Ask to see a portfolio of work. Look for the artist's strengths. Remember, an artist who works well in oil paints does not necessarily work well in cut paper. If you want to use cut paper, this artist may not be for you. Know what you want and look for the artist who can do it. Also note that if a renderer works well in publication design, that same person may not be able to produce usable 35mm slides.

Give the rendering artist specific and clear direction. Your thumbnail sketch may need to be clarified. Specify color, layout, type size and style, rendering medium, and the like. Be sure the renderer understands the directions. Do not be ambiguous or vague. To assure that he or she understands, ask to have the directions repeated from the artist's point of view. Clear directions can lead to a usable product. Vague directions could lead to well-laid out visuals that are not usable. Time is usually a major factor. Be realistic about the amount of time a job should take, and then give the artist the time in which to do it.

Artists who render visual aids for learning must be willing to take direction from the educational message designer. That is, a visual display needs to embody good graphic design qualities and contribute to the learning of the audience. To do this you need teamwork and cooperation. Both the conceptualizer and the renderer must be willing to return to the drawing board to rethink and re-do the visual plan and/or the visual product. Visual thinking is a process that requires exercising your skills and expanding your repertoire. Educational message designers and renderers must work together to generate original, well-conceived visualizations that can improve as well as inspire learning.

Notes

Appendix

Glossary

A

Arbitrary symbol. A visual element that is purely geometric or abstract. Used to represent an object or group of objects.

Aspect ratio. The relationship of the height to the width of a visual frame. Expressed as a ratio (e.g., 3 units high by 4 wide is expressed 3:4).

Auditory learning. Learning that occurs primarily through the sense of hearing. Auditory learners retain information that is presented verbally with more facility than information presented visually or through the sense of touch.

B

Bleed. The effect produced when a visual element continues to the edge of the frame, giving the impression it continues beyond the edge.

C

Clarity. A set of visual design considerations concerned with whether a visual is clear, easy to interpret, and to the point.

Complex visuals. Visuals that require intricate effects such as animation of many images or a single complex image. Detailed, visually rich screens or pages. Non-repetitive, complex images.

Concept-related symbol. A visual element designed to represent the essence of an object or group of objects. Concept-related symbols lack the detail found in image-related symbols.

Conceptualize. The intellectual process of inventing visual and/or verbal symbols to communicate a message. To create a storyboard, rough draft, sketch, or mockup. This process involves both thought and visual design skills.

Course developer. The person in a course development effort who is responsible for the design, development, and production of all educational materials.

D

Degrees of visualization. A system that categorizes visuals along a continuum from purely verbal images (called Type I) to purely visual images (called Type VII).

Developmental test. A test performed on all course materials prior to production of the materials. This test is performed with a sample of the target audience.

Dynamic layout. An unbalanced layout in which a visual is divided in half vertically and the elements are primarily right or left of the dividing line.

E

Emphasized pictorial frame. A Type VI frame contains only visual symbols. The message is emphasized through techniques such as arrows or shading.

Emphasized reader frame. A Type II frame composed mainly of text with a visual technique used to direct the viewer's attention.

Emphasizing technique. Graphic technique used to draw attention to an element of a visual. See also Highlighting.

F

Figure/ground relationship. The contrast between the information being presented in the foreground (called the figure) of a visual, and the background (or ground).

Formal layout. A balanced layout in which the frame is divided in half vertically, and images are balanced equally on either side of the dividing line.

Frame. The space containing the elements of a visual. The size and shape (aspect ratio) of a frame are determined by the delivery system used to present the visual.

G

Graph formal. One of five basic ways to present tabular data: line, bar, circle, pictorial, or map/area.

Graphic artist. One who renders conceptualizations into finished art.

Graphic symbol. A symbol using simple, bold, shape-oriented images to represent something. See Image-related symbol, Concept-related symbol, and Arbitrary symbol.

H

Highlighting. The use of graphic techniques (shading, blowup, arrows, circles, color, etc.) to emphasize an aspect of the message in a visual.

I

Illustration. A realistic, detailed drawing of an object.

Image-related symbol. A symbol designed to represent an object in a highly recognizable form, often taking the form of an accurate silhouette or profile.

Imagination. A set of visual design considerations concerned with whether a visual is compelling to the audience.

Informal layout. A layout in which the frame is divided in half vertically with equal amounts of visual elements on each side of the dividing line, but not placed in the same plane.

Instructional design. The process of planning lessons based on learning objectives.

Instructional designer. One who designs lessons, courses, or educational presentations.

K

Kinds of visuals. A system that categorizes visual elements along a continuum from concrete to abstract images.

Kinesthetic learning. Learning that occurs primarily through the sense of touch. Kinesthetic learners retain tactile information with more facility than information presented visually or through the sense of hearing.

L

Learning environment. A set of conditions, including physical space, technology employed, or other factors used in the delivery of education.

M

Margin. The space around the edge of a visual frame.

Media specialist. A person who has expertise in the use of various media for the delivery of education.

P

Pan. Camera motion used to produce the horizontal movement of words or images across the viewer's field of vision. Primarily a film/video term.

Pictorial frame. A Type VII frame in which visual elements carry the entire message.

Pictorial frame with verbal cues. A Type V frame composed primarily of visual symbols with words used to label new or exotic phenomena.

Pictorial symbol. A visual image that uses photographs or illustrations to represent an object or group of objects (usually a realistic representation).

Pilot testing. A way to try out a visual idea. Used to validate a concept during developmental testing.

Progressive disclosure. A presentation technique in which elements of a message are revealed in sequence, building the message until the entire message is revealed.

R

Reader frame. A Type I visual composed of text only.

Reader frame with visual cues. A Type III frame composed primarily of verbal elements but including pictorial or graphic symbols that help communicate the message.

Render. The process that turns a conceptualized message into a usable finished product. To prepare, record, or construct finished art.

Rough sketch. A preliminary sketch of a visual idea, used to evaluate the concept of the visual with peers.

S

Storyboard. A visual planning device used to communicate visual ideas and notes for production of the final visual.

Subject matter expert. A content specialist. Responsible for technical accuracy and credibility of information.

Symbol. Something that represents something else by association, resemblance, or convention; in particular, an object used to represent something invisible. See also Pictorial symbol, Graphic symbol, Verbal symbol.

T

Thumbnail sketch. A small, quick, rendered drawing.

Tilting. Camera motion used to produce the vertical movement of words or images across the viewer's field of vision. Primarily a film/video term.

U

Unity. A set of visual design considerations concerned with whether a visual is composed in a manner that unifies the elements of the individual visual.

V

Verbal symbol. Words used to describe an object or thing.

Verbal/visual balanced frame. A Type IV frame in which verbal and visual elements carry the message with equal weight.

Verbal/visual continuum. The scale used to classify images into seven categories (known as Types) according to their relative use of verbal and visual techniques. See also Degrees of visualization.

Verbalization. The process of using words to describe and represent objects, concepts, or feelings.

Visual. Any projected or printed set of images designed to communicate a message or information.

Visual aid. A pictorial or graphic representation of information intended to communicate.

Visual element. Any single image or part of an image in a visual.

Visual learning. Learning that occurs primarily through the sense of sight. Visual learners retain information that is presented visually with more facility than information presented through the sense of touch or hearing.

Visual literacy. The ability to "read," interpret, and understand information presented in pictorial or graphic images.

Visual thinking. The ability to turn information of all types into pictures, graphics, or forms that help communicate the information.

Visual weight. The relative size and boldness of an image or element. The more one image stands out from others, the more visual weight it is said to have.

Visualization. The process of designing and developing a visual concept. The process of graphically or pictorially representing objects, concepts, or feelings.

Storyboard Form
35mm slides (2:3 aspect ratio)

Visual Name _____

Frame # _____

Key Learning Point _____
_____
_____

Production Notes _____
_____
_____
_____
_____
_____

Script/Prompting Notes _____
_____
_____
_____
_____

Storyboard Form
Flip Chart (4:3 aspect ratio)

Visual Name _____

Frame # _____

Key Learning Point _____
_____
_____

Production Notes _____
_____
_____
_____
_____

Script/Prompting Notes _____
_____
_____
_____
_____
_____

Storyboard Form
Overhead Transparency (4:5 aspect ratio)

Visual Name _____

Frame # _____ Media Type _____

Key Learning Point _____
_____
_____

Production Notes _____
_____
_____
_____
_____

Script/Prompting Notes _____
_____
_____
_____
_____

117

Storyboard Form
Video, Computer, Television, and Film (3:4 aspect ratio)

Visual Name _____

Frame # _____ **Media Type** _____

Key Learning Point _____
_____
_____

Production Notes _____
_____
_____
_____
_____
_____

Script/Prompting Notes _____
_____
_____
_____
_____
_____

Storyboard Card

#

Production Notes:

Authoring Notes:

Visual

Script:

VISUAL DESIGN CONSIDERATIONS
Is the visual clear?

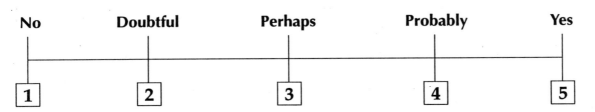

No	Doubtful	Perhaps	Probably	Yes
1	2	3	4	5

1. Are the words and images LARGE ENOUGH to see?

| 1 | 2 | 3 | 4 | 5 |

2. Are the words and images BOLD ENOUGH to see?

| 1 | 2 | 3 | 4 | 5 |

3. Is there a GOOD CONTRAST between figure and ground?

| 1 | 2 | 3 | 4 | 5 |

4. Is the visual APPROPRIATE for the intended audience?

| 1 | 2 | 3 | 4 | 5 |

5. What VISUAL DEVICES are used to direct the viewer's attention?

| 1 | 2 | 3 | 4 | 5 |

6. Does the visual contain only the ESSENTIAL INFORMATION?

| 1 | 2 | 3 | 4 | 5 |

7. Are appropriate visual SEQUENCING TECHNIQUES used to present complex ideas?

| 1 | 2 | 3 | 4 | 5 |

VISUAL DESIGN CONSIDERATIONS
Is the visual well composed?

UNITY

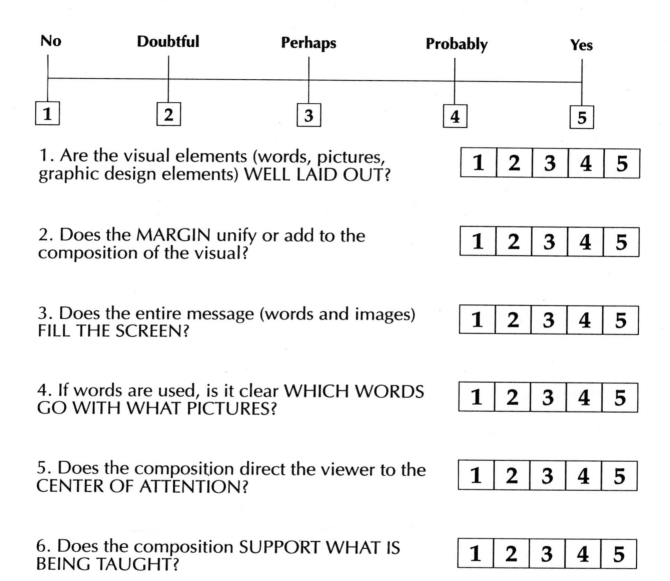

No	Doubtful	Perhaps	Probably	Yes
1	2	3	4	5

1. Are the visual elements (words, pictures, graphic design elements) WELL LAID OUT?

1	2	3	4	5

2. Does the MARGIN unify or add to the composition of the visual?

1	2	3	4	5

3. Does the entire message (words and images) FILL THE SCREEN?

1	2	3	4	5

4. If words are used, is it clear WHICH WORDS GO WITH WHAT PICTURES?

1	2	3	4	5

5. Does the composition direct the viewer to the CENTER OF ATTENTION?

1	2	3	4	5

6. Does the composition SUPPORT WHAT IS BEING TAUGHT?

1	2	3	4	5

VISUAL DESIGN CONSIDERATIONS
Is the visual compelling?

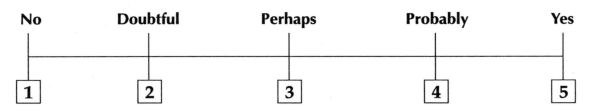

No	Doubtful	Perhaps	Probably	Yes
1	2	3	4	5

1. Does the visual "connect" to THE LEARNER'S EXISTING KNOWLEDGE and interest?

1	2	3	4	5

2. Does the visual have STYLE THAT RELATES to the other visuals being used in the lesson?

1	2	3	4	5

3. Does the visual GAIN THE ATTENTION of the viewer?

1	2	3	4	5

4. Does the visual HOLD THE ATTENTION of the viewer?

1	2	3	4	5

5. Does the visual present the information in a way that helps the viewer REMEMBER that information?

1	2	3	4	5

Annotated Bibliography

Alexander, Mary Jean. *Handbook of Decorative Design and Ornament.* New York: Tudor Publishing. 1965. 128p.

   Treats design as decoration. First chapter summarizes general principles of design. Remainder of book consists of examples of decorative art: bands and borders, architectural embellishment, repeat patterns, and historic ornament of different periods and cultures. A sourcebook for ideas and patterns.

Arnheim, Rudolf. *Visual Thinking.* Berkeley: University of California Press. 1969. 345p.

   An erudite and readable book that has become a seminal work on the importance of visual thinking. Arnheim, a professor of art, posits that all thinking is perceptual in nature, that thinking and sensing require the same cognitive operations. Seeks to define the concept of abstraction and the relationship of thought to pictures, symbols, and signs. The final chapter is a discussion of how the theory applies to education.

Bain, Eric K. *The Theory and Practice of Typographic Design.* New York: Hastings House. 1970. 182p.

   A practical, easy-to-use guide to the principles that underlie display typography. Intended to foster a critical appreciation of the art of type design, not necessarily the ability to practice it. Organized from elementary to advanced levels of technique.

Baird, Russell N., Arthur T. Turnbull, and Duncan McDonald. *The Graphics of Communication.* 5th edition. New York: Holt, Rinehart, and Winston. 1987. 391p.

   A straightforward textbook on graphic design written for journalism students. Brings together communication theory and computer technology under the premise that the new technologies are predicated on human information processing. Practical information on creating visual and verbal copy for production, with lengthy treatments on the use of type and pictures. Final chapter is a brief history of graphic communication.

Balkam, Keith and Richard Mills. *Starting Graphics and Design.* London: Heinemann Educational Books. 1984. 80p.

   A beginner's book for teaching high school students to develop graphic and design skills. Starts with simple line drawing, but moves rapidly into advanced techniques of depicting motion and mechanisms. Includes several exercises for each skill.

Ballinger, Raymond A. *Design with Paper in Art and Graphic Design.* New York: Van Nostrand Reinhold. 1982. 144p.

   A novel look at creative uses of paper in graphic design. Techniques include paper cutting, folding, and embossing, with applications to art and commercial purposes. Examples include cards, brochures, advertisements, sculpture, pop-up books, and masks. An idea book for those interested in three-dimensional effects.

Ballinger, Raymond A. *Layout and Graphic Design.* New York: Van Nostrand Reinhold. 1970. 96p.

Designed to give students of graphic arts a foundation in all aspects of layout–including symmetry, page size, typeface, and use of borders, halftones, and line art. Profusely illustrated, with assignments and exercises for stimulation and practice.

Bang, Molly. *Picture This: Perception and Composition.* Boston: Little Brown. 1991. 141p.

A truly insightful little book about how pictures convey emotion. Using simple shapes and minimal color, Bang constructs a Red Riding Hood picture that embodies all the feelings of the tale. Each choice is analyzed for why it works. The second half of the book presents basic principles of composition and the emotions they evoke. A profoundly simple book that both precedes and transcends other books on graphic arts theory.

Beach, Mark, Steve Shepro, and Ken Russon. *Getting It Printed.* Portland, Oregon: Coast to Coast Books. 1986. 236p.

A handbook about the production end of graphic design, developed for those who oversee the printing of graphic arts materials. This book may also prove useful to those seeking to understand the technical specifications that define the printing industry; for example, type fonts, grades of paper, inks, bindings, and printing methods. Glossary included.

Beakley, George C. *Freehand Drawing and Visualization.* Indianapolis: Bobbs-Merrill. 1982. 85p.

A how-to book for visualizing and sketching. Assumes a persuasive tone to instill in the reader a positive attitude toward drawing, then provides detailed instruction and activities to increase visualization skills. Exercises on the use of depth, perspective, value and light, contrast, and space. Can be used for group or independent study.

Beatty, LaMond F. *Still Pictures.* Instructional Media Library. Vol. 14. Englewood Cliffs, New Jersey: Educational Technology Publications. 1981. 103p.

Specific directions on the use of still pictures–study prints, photographs, textbook illustrations, and clip art in educational lessons, with a discussion of the advantages and disadvantages of each type. Discusses the application of design principles in preparation and use of pictures. Also provides information on the preservation and storage of pictures. Sparsely illustrated.

Berryman, Gregg. *Notes on Graphic Design and Visual Communication.* Los Altos, California: William Kaufmann. 1984. 46p.

A short, hand-lettered monograph that provides orientation to the field of graphic design. Discusses basic elements of design in a simple, crisp style. Explains alternative directions the design process can take, e.g., linear, cyclical, branching. Special attention given to symbols, logos, typography, and grid work.

Bettmann Portable Archive. New York: Picture House Press. 1966. 229p.

A sample of materials from the files of the Bettmann Archive, a library of pictures from the past. The files include old photographs, illustrations from posters and handbills, and other printed materials that constitute a treasure trove of information about how things used to look, how they were made, and how people thought about them. Indexed by subject and by idea or image. Although the samples are small in size, they are useful to stimulate the imagination or to fill the need for a particular image.

Biggs, John R. *Letter-forms & Lettering.* Poole, England: Blanford Press. 1977. 128p.

Takes the approach that letters are things as well as symbols. Examines the composition of the Latin alphabet as lines and curves, then compares it with other alphabets and ideographic systems. Provides exercises in experimenting with line and legibility. Some discussion of typeface design. Boldly illustrated.

Bockus, H. William, Jr. *Advertising Graphics.* 4th edition. New York: Macmillan. 1986. 241p.

A reference and workbook for the advertising artist. Discusses tools, design elements, and production processes. Draws in pertinent philosophies from the fields of art, economics, and education. Several design problems are put forward to simulate experience in layout and production. Book itself is a visual exercise with widely varied page format and typography.

Booth-Clibborn, Edward and Daniele Baroni. *The Language of Graphics.* New York: Harry N. Abrams. 1979. 320p.

A voluminous compendium of applied graphic art. Editorial, advertising, and illustrated news graphics are all represented. Includes a discussion of three-dimensional graphic art as applied to packaging, games, fashion, and origami. Text examines significance of the sign and its psychological effects, but this is really a "coffee table book" to browse for graphic ideas.

Borgman, Harry. *Advertising Layout Techniques.* New York: Watson-Guptill. 1983. 143p.

Intended for advertisers, this book traces the evolution of thought processes through several advertising assignments. Examples present stages of layout from rough sketch to finished product. The author demonstrates how the choice of medium (marker, wax pencil, gouache, acrylics) affect the layout and what it communicates. Practice lessons included.

Bowman, William J. *Graphic Communication.* New York: John Wiley and Sons. 1968. 210p.

A book of solutions to a variety of recurrent problems in graphic communication. Explores (1) the graphic figure as a communications medium; (2) visual language as it applies to graphic design; and (3) principles and procedures for visualization. Includes a library of graphic art to help answer basic questions of design. Uses simple pencil drawings to show alternative ways to depict design concepts.

Bragonier, Reginald, Jr. and David Fisher. *What's What: A Visual Glossary of the Physical World.* Maplewood, New Jersey: Hammond. 1981. 565p.

An entertaining and enlightening dictionary of everyday objects, pictorially represented by line drawings or photographs. Access is possible by subject or by name of part. Useful for locating proper terminology or for browsing.

Brown, James W., Richard B. Lewis, and Fred F. Harcleroad. *AV Instruction: Technology, Media, and Methods.* 6th edition. New York: McGraw-Hill. 1983. 528p.

A comprehensive standard textbook on the production and use of audiovisual (AV) materials for instruction, organized by type of media. Includes supplementary information on operation of AV equipment, duplication processes, and physical facilities. Offers a broad, if not deep, portrait of AV technology.

Burns, Aaron. *Typography.* New York: Reinhold Publishing. 1961. 111p.

Typographic examples shown in full-page advertising spreads. The back of the book is devoted to explanations of how each example was designed and used, with attention to any special techniques employed. Emphasis on the unorthodox and experimental use of type. Examples are a bit dated, but the analyses remain valuable.

Burtt, George. *Putting Yourself Across with the Art of Graphic Persuasion.* West Nyack, New York: Parker Publishing Co. 1972. 242p.

A layman's guide to simple art techniques that enhance communication skills. Emphasizes visual presentation as the expression of a personal style for a specific purpose. Presents simple and practical methods for getting ideas across, simplifying information, and using art methods to illustrate, dramatize, and demonstrate meaning. Includes tips on lettering, cartooning, making charts and graphs, and photography.

Cabibi, John F.J. *Copy Preparation for Printing.* New York: McGraw-Hill. 1973. 152p.

Guide to preparing camera-ready copy. Presents fundamentals of typography, copyfitting, manuscript preparation, and advertising psychology.

Cataldo, John W. *Graphic Design and Visual Communication.* Scranton, Pennsylvania: International Textbook Company. 1966. 293p.

Explores idea of graphic design as social art. Seminal message is the fusion of form and content to create meaning. Deals with typography, visual-verbal language, and graphic forms of pictorial expression. Book itself is a mix of graphic forms with a text dwarfed by photos and illustrations.

Chermayeff, Ivan. *The Design Necessity.* Cambridge, Massachusetts: MIT Press. 1973. 80p.

Casebook of 15 federally initiated design projects in the areas of visual communication, interiors and industrial design, architecture, and landscape environment. Examples are somewhat dated, but text presents cogent argument that design is necessary, not ornamental, in meeting human needs.

Complete Catalog of Dover Books. Mineola, New York: Dover Publications. 1988. 64p.

> Annotated list of titles from Dover Publications. Includes a wide selection of inexpensive softcover books on design with ready-to-use illustrations and reproducible clip art in the public domain. The illustrations are of good quality and cover numerous subjects. In addition to the general catalog, some catalogs are available for specific subject areas. A wonderland of ideas from many subject areas and periods.

Cook, Alton and Robert Fleury. *Type & Color: A Handbook of Creative Combinations.* Rockport, Massachusetts: Rockport Publishers. 1989. 157p.

> Explores the use of color in selecting type and background, as an alternative to traditional black-on-white design. Invites experimentation with color through the use of acetate sheets, each with four typefaces, which may be overlaid on bands of color in varying shades and hues. Good resource for playing with possibilities.

Corbeil, Jean Claude. *The Facts on File Visual Dictionary.* New York: Facts on File Publications. 1986. 797p.

> A reference that allows the reader to look up the name of an image through its picture. Provides a visual glossary for the vocabulary of everyday life in industrialized cultures. Illustrations are line drawings with all visible parts labled. Organized by subject field with general, thematic, and specialized indexes.

Cossette, Claude. *How Pictures Speak: A Brief Introduction to Iconics.* Paper presented at the 32nd International Communications Association Conference, Boston, Massachusetts, May 1-5, 1982. Quebec: Les Editors Riguil International. 1982. 45p.

> A small paper that explores a narrow definition of pictures as strictly functional rather than aesthetic. Discusses iconics, the development of graphic symbols, and how people analyze pictures. Introduces a system for analyzing and rating pictures based on what and how they communicate.

Craig, James. *Phototypesetting: A Design Manual.* New York: Watson-Guptill. 1990. 189p.

> This book is more about typography than phototypesetting, with fully two-thirds of its pages devoted to a presentation of basic typographic vocabulary. Each term is accompanied by a multitude of examples which not only provide illustration, but also help train the eye in the aesthetics of typographic use. All aspects of typesetting, design, and copyfitting are profusely represented.

Crow, Wendell C. *Communication Graphics.* Englewood Cliffs, New Jersey: Prentice-Hall. 1986. 322p.

> A textbook approach to the mechanics of graphic arts in the printing industry. Chapters of interest are those dealing with the design process, typographic and graphic images, and color.

Croy, Peter. *Graphic Design and Reproduction Techniques.* New York: Hastings House. 1968. 282p.

An encyclopedic reference on printing processes–letterpress, planographic, intaglio, craft, and silk screen. Written for graphic artists to answer questons about technical aspects and practical problems of design and production. Also covers typography, book design illustrations, technical drawings, photography, lettering, and air brushing. Valuable ready reference.

Dennis, Ervin A. and John D. Jenkins. *Comprehensive Graphic Arts.* 2nd edition. Indianapolis: Bobbs-Merrill. 1983. 605p.

Emphasis on book production, with detailed illustrated explanations of printing processes. Preliminary chapters offer a succinct explanation of design principles. Includes descriptions of book finishing and binding and choices of paper and ink. Also presents information on peripheral topics such as dark room procedures and legal constraints on publishing.

Diethelm, Walter J. *Form and Communication.* Zurich: ABC Edition. 1974. 227p.

Stimulating examples of graphic design in a variety of media and formats, including symbols and sources with historic reference. A beautiful book of graphic design solutions to problems in industry, marketing, and communication. English text is a rather awkward and stilted translation but the designs are stunning.

Dondis, Donis A. *A Primer of Visual Literacy.* Cambridge, Massachusetts: MIT Press. 1973. 194p.

Basic theoretical background about visual communication and expression. Considers visual language as analogous to verbal language. Emphasis on developing the viewer's ability to interpret visually. Defines basic elements of visual communication, visual techniques and styles, psychological and physiological implications of creative composition, and the range of media and formats that are properly called visual. Includes exercises.

Dreyfuss, Henry. *Symbol Sourcebook.* New York: McGraw-Hill. 1972. 292p.

An extensive data bank of graphic symbols in use around the world, organized first by discipline, then by graphic form, then by meaning. The table of contents, printed in 18 languages, reflects the international perspective of the book. Fosters the movement toward standardized, universally understandable graphic symbols, specifically those that give instruction, directions, and warnings. Also has a section on the varied meaning of colors as symbols. A rich resource that is sensitive to symbol, meaning, and culture.

Dwyer, Francis M. *A Guide for Improving Visualized Instruction.* State College, Pennsylvania: Learning Services. 1972. 138p.

Cites need for empirical validation of effectiveness of AV instructional materials. Reviews research findings about human learning in visual instruction with slides, television, programmed instruction, and textbooks. Includes model for evaluating impact and effectiveness of AV materials. Dated, but one of the few documents with research orientation.

Easterby, Ronald and Harm Zwaga, eds. *Information Design: The Design and Evaluation of Signs and Printed Material*. Chichester, New York: John Wiley and Sons. 1984. 588p.

A compilation of 29 papers from a conference on the visual presentation of information. Papers represent a broad range of disciplines with a common research interest in visual perception. Relates research to practice in those areas of study not strictly allied to computer technology; for example, the papers consider the design of public information signs, road signs, instructional materials, forms, and questionnaires. Among the applications discussed are the design of instructional materials and the use of space and structure in instructional texts.

Edwards, Betty. *Drawing on the Artist Within*. New York: Simon and Schuster. 1986. 240p.

An expansion of Edward's earlier work, based on the notion of visual language as a grammar of drawing. The author gently guides the reader into using the right side of the brain to express itself in drawing. Tone is relaxed and contemplative. Step-by-step exercises are provided.

Edwards, Betty. *Drawing on the Right Side of the Brain*. Los Angeles: J.P. Tarcher. 1979. 207p.

Popular introduction to drawing, based on the author's teaching experience and theories of right vs. left brain functions. Seeks to instill confidence and control artistic expression through a series of psychological and artistic exercises. Many examples, including some impressive success stories.

Faruque, Omar. *Graphic Communication as a Design Tool*. New York: Van Nostrand Reinhold. 1984. 218p.

Considers design concepts in light of contemporary views on problem-solving, visual thinking, perception, and research on the human brain and creativity. Heavily illustrated, mostly with architectural sketches.

Feldman, Edmund Burke. *Varieties of Visual Experience*. New York: Harry N. Abrams. 1987. 528p.

The third section of this book, "The Structure of Art," is a well-illustrated introduction to the elements of visual perception and their use in art. Examples are drawn from the fine arts, with an emphasis on contemporary works. The rest of the book deals mainly with issues in art appreciation.

Felten, Charles J. *Layout 4: Printing, Design and Typography*. St. Petersburg, Florida: Charles J. Felten Publishers. 1970. 303p.

Compilation of author's articles on printing and design. Sample topics include copy analysis, layout formats, design tools and techniques, and the use of supplemental art. Shows how advertising and printing can be made attractive, interesting, and easy to read. Graphic examples are pedestrian, but articles on specific topics may prove useful.

Fineman, Mark. *The Inquisitive Eye*. New York: Oxford University Press. 1981. 171p.

Scientific theory about the physiology and psychology of visual perception explained for the layperson. Deals with how the visual is experienced and how the eye responds to visual stimuli. Many examples of optical illusions in full-page black-and-white illustration.

Fleming, Malcolm L. ed. *Aspects of Perception: Their Relation to Instructional Communications*. Bloomington, Indiana: School of Education, Indiana University. 1971. 216p.

Proceedings of an interdisciplinary conference on human perception. Includes eleven papers, two of which deal directly with visual perception. One explores the concept of visual literacy; the other presents research studies on children's responses to television and motion picture viewing. Other papers also include some discussion of visual perception.

Friedman, Mildred. *Graphic Design in America: A Visual Language History*. New York: Harry N. Abrams. 1989. 264p.

A catalog from a 1989 exhibition of American graphic design in the twentieth centry at the Walker Art Center in Minneapolis. The historical perspective is developed through essays by noted designers who correlate graphic art with social and political climate. Also included are interviews with innovative graphic artists and commentary on current trends.

Gardner, William. *Alphabet at Work*. New York: St. Martin's Press. 1982. 112p.

A practical examination of the alphabet and its applications. Critique of each letter in the Latin alphabet, describing its attributes and how it is best displayed. Gives guidelines and examples for letter spacing. Explores a variety of alphabetical uses with abundant examples of both serious and fanciful applications.

Garvey, Mona. *Teaching Displays: Their Purpose, Construction, and Use*. Hamden, Connecticut: Linnet Press. 1972. 128p.

Resource book for teachers on the purposes and methods of creating visual displays. Presupposes no artistic training or access to production facilities. Simple examples of handmade lettering and images. Classroom-oriented.

Gikow, Jacqueline. *Graphic Illustration in Black and White*. New York: Design Press. 1991. 143p.

Focuses on monochromatic illustration including drawings, silhouettes, and photographs. Chapters three through six offer sound advice on the use of media and varied techniques. The discussion is practical and assign-ment-oriented with exercises provided. Illustrations are plentiful and aptly chosen. Can be used as a guide for self-instruction.

Gill, Bob. *Forget All the Rules You Ever Learned About Graphic Design, Including the Ones in This Book*. New York: Watson-Guptill. 1981. 167p.

Gill maintains that unique graphic designs are generated by considering the design problem in a unique way. This book is an illustration of that principle, with each page a design assignment (usually from advertising) that is redefined and solved with a fresh approach. Offers insight into the creative thinking of the graphic artist.

Gombrich, E.H., Julian Hochberg, and Max Black. *Art, Perception and Reality*. Baltimore: Johns Hopkins University Press. 1972. 132p.

Three essays on the nature of representation in art. The first discusses the perception of physical likeness in the human face; the second argues that perception is skilled, purposeful behavior; the third is a critical look at theories describing how pictures are represented. Illustrated.

Graves, Maitland. *The Art of Color and Design.* New York: McGraw-Hill. 1951. 439p.

An old but enduring introduction to the principles of color and design. Sound treatment of proportion, color, texture, and harmony–with classic examples throughout. Includes exercises.

Hagen, Margaret A. *The Perception of Pictures: Volume II. Durer's Devices: Beyond the Projective Model of Pictures.* New York: Academic Press. 1980. 356p.

A collection of papers that reports basic research on the perception of pictures, conducted primarily with special populations such as the blind and the neurologically impaired. Includes discussion of theories of perception. A scholarly book, densely written.

Hamilton, Edward. *Graphic Design for the Computer Age.* New York: Van Nostrand Reinhold. 1970. 191p.

A discussion of the evolution of graphic design up to 1970. Includes movements in popular culture, the impact of technology, and other societal factors that influence communication design. The author borrows his narrative style and striking illustrations from the Time-Life books, of which he is former art director.

Hanks, Kurt and Larry Belliston. *Draw! A Visual Approach to Thinking, Learning, and Communicating.* Los Altos, California: William Kaufmann. 1977. 242p.

Discusses drawing as a collaboration of the brain, eye, hand, and image. Presents 19 specific methods, tools, and techniques for drawing–each accompanied by large, pertinent illustrations. Encourages "rapid visualization" of fleeting ideas and drawing as an aid to creativity, memory, and communication. Illustrations and exercises are plentiful.

Hartley, James. *Designing Instructional Text.* 2nd edition. New York: Nichols Publishing. 1985. 175p.

Focuses on the presentation of text in instructional materials. Offers guidelines based on current practice and relevant research. Topics include typographic planning, selection of page size, writing of text, role of illustrations, and effective layout for forms and questionnaires. Provides several examples of text before and after revision. Helpful for desktop publishers.

Heinich, Robert, Michael Molenda, and James D. Russell. *Instructional Media and the New Technologies of Instruction.* 3rd edition. New York: Macmillan. 1989. 456p.

A comprehensive textbook on AV instructional media, their design, use, and social impact. A broad overview, organized by media type. Chapter Three examines visual literacy as it applies to learning processes and use of visual media. Extends presentation to include technology of teleconferencing and interactive video.

Henrion, F.H.K. *Top Graphic Design*. New York: Zurich: ABC Edition. 1983. 159p.

Presents examples of graphic art by 18 leading designers of international renown. The intent is to compile visual communications that use cliché and symbol in a provocative and experimental way. The selections are varied but share a bold and dramatic approach. Includes a brief biography and comment by each designer.

Herdeg, Walter, ed. *Graphis/Diagrams*. Zurich: The Graphis Press. 1974. 183p.

An international collection of fine examples of graphic art that depicts abstract facts or functions. Its diagrams, charts, timetables, graphs, and maps exemplify visual thinking that ranges from the practical to the extravagant, but is always elegantly executed. Examples are grouped by function or concept. An index provides access by type of diagram. A beautiful book for stimulation and inspiration.

Hinrichs, Kit and Delphine Hirasuna, eds. *Stars and Stripes*. San Francisco: Chronicle Books. 1987. 107p.

Personal interpretations of the American flag by 96 designers and graphic artists. Each entry is beautifully reproduced, one to a page, accompanied by a brief vita of the artist. Entries reflect a wide variety of media and messages that are comic, ironic, elegant, fanciful. For creative stimulation.

Holmes, Nigel. *Designer's Guide to Creating Charts and Diagrams*. New York: Watson-Guptill. 1984. 192p.

In-depth examination of four types of charts: line, bar, pie, and table. Considers appropriate and inappropriate uses of each type. Nine step-by-step examples of the process of designing charts suitable for given data. Also includes library of well-designed charts. The Text is informative, but this book really teaches through visual example. Gloriously illustrated.

Horn, George. *How to Prepare Visual Materials for School Use*. Worcester, Massachusetts: Davis Publications. 1963. 73p.

Resourceful and sometimes ingenious use of everyday objects for instructional displays in schools. Devices for visual presentation include boxes, window shades, mailing tubes, and clotheslines. Text is sparse; examples are simply drawn.

Hornung, Clarence P. *Handbook of Designs and Devices*. New York: Dover. 1946. 216p.

First published sixty years ago (Harper and Brothers, 1932), this collection of graphic designs remains a valuable sourcebook. Each section presents a basic shape in illustrations that progress from simple to more elaborate forms. The designs, many drawn from ancient cultures, are embellished or decorated to stimulate the imagination. The back of the book contains notes that give a verbal description of each design, its meaning, and its history.

Houghton, H.A. and D.M. Willows. *Instructional Issues.* New York: Springer-Verlag, 1987. 196p. Vol. 2 of The Psychology of Illustration.

The second volume of a set, this book considers historical and pragmatic issues related to the use of illustration in textbooks and other instructional materials. Intended both as a handbook for practitioners in instructional design and as a guide on practical matters related to the use and production of illustrated text. Includes reported research on the use of illustrated textbooks, an analytical model for consideration of illustrated materials, and a discussion of the impact of computer graphics. See also: Willows, D.M. and H.A. Houghton. *Basic Research.* Vol. 1 of The Psychology of Illustration.

Hurlburt, Allen. *Layout: The Design of the Printed Page.* New York: Watson-Guptill. 1977. 159p.

An analysis of page layout as it is rooted in 20th century art movements. Considers (1) the forces that contribute to style; (2) elements that create design; (3) image and word content that give meaning to design; and (4) designs that evoke response. Teaches by analysis of examples.

Hurley, Gerald D. and Angus McDougall. *Visual Impact in Print: How to Make Pictures Communicate.* Chicago: American Publishers Press. 1971. 208p.

Guide to photojournalism for photographers, editors, and designers. Shows how communication through still photos can be improved by good editing. Rich in examples with illuminating commentary.

Hurrell, Ron. *The Thames and Hudson Manual of Television Graphics.* London: Thames and Hudson. 1973. 136p.

Manual for developing visual symbols for the television screen. Covers topics of lettering, captions, photography, titling, and animation. The technologies in the book have been surpassed, but the discussion of principles remains current. Practical slant, with abundant examples.

Jones, Gerre. *How to Prepare Professional Design Brochures.* New York: McGraw-Hill. 1976. 277p.

Although intended for those who prepare brochures for architectural and engineering firms, this is nonetheless a comprehensive and economically written handbook for any brochure designer. Inclusive treatment of all aspects of brochure production, with detailed specifications on type, format, and layout. Direct, business writing style that incorporates basic design elements into a discussion of the practical purposes and processes of brochure production.

Karo, Jerzy. *Graphic Design: Problems, Methods, and Solutions.* New York: Van Nostrand Reinhold. 1975. 108p.

Assumes an advertising perspective that treats graphic art as persuasion. Poses a series of graphic problems, ranging from the simple to the complex, then analyzes methods and rationale for solutions. Examples reflect a variety of messages and audiences. Several approaches to design are illustrated; e.g., allegorical, direct, dramatic, emotive, illustrative, symbolic, whimsical.

Kidron, Michael and Ronald Segal. *The State of the World Atlas*. New York: Simon and Schuster. 1991. 159p.

Shows how maps can be used to depict a wide variety of information through the creative use of shape, symbol, color, size, and insets. Consists entirely of maps diverse in design and purpose, many intentionally distorted to illustrate bias or inequity. Explanatory notes included in the back of the book. For alternatives to traditional map design.

Kince, Eli. *Visual Puns in Design: The Pun Used as a Communications Tool*. New York: Watson-Guptill. 1982. 168p.

An illustrated definition of the pun as a visual device. For the graphic designer looking for graphic solutions that are surprising or humorous. Discussion of how visual messages can touch on different levels of meaning in unexpected ways. Heart of the book is its collection of visual puns that range from the whimsical to the grotesque.

Koch, Rudolf. *The Book of Signs*. New York: Dover. 1930. 103p.

A book of 493 symbols used by primitive peoples and early Christians, collected from carvings, inscriptions, and manuscripts, and reproduced from woodcuts. Text, printed in Gothic type, gives brief explanation of meaning and relationship among the symbols.

Kostelanetz, Richard. *Visual Language*. Brooklyn, New York: Assembling Press. 1970. 30p.

Consists entirely of letters and words arranged to form picture messages. Author contends that words may be more expressive as concrete images than as verbal symbols. A book more to intrigue than to inform.

Kroehl, Heinz. *Communication Design 2000*. Zurich: ABC Edition. 1987. 204p.

The commentary in this book winds around examples of bold, slick advertising from around the world that are dramatic and avant garde. The text, in English, French and German is rooted in semiotic theory and seeks to establish a philosophy of graphic art that extends into the next century. The discussion is highly abstract, but the designs may prove useful for stimulation.

Kuwayama, Yasaburo. *Volume One: Trademarks & Symbols of the World–The Alphabet in Design*. Rockport, Massachusetts: Rockport Publishers. 1988. 207p.

An international compilation of logos based on alphabetic design. The logos are arranged alphabetically and each is coded to an index which lists its business, designer, client, year, and color. The designs vary widely in degree of abstraction and offer imaginative uses of the alphabet design for advertising purposes.

Landa, Robin. *Visual Solutions*. Englewood Cliffs, New Jersey: Prentice-Hall. 1986. 222p.

Workbook of projects to expand creativity through design experience. Assignments on color, typography, graphics, illustration, advertising design, conceptual and perceptual art, and storyboards. Gives examples of works by professional artists with brief comments.

Levie, W. Howard. *Research on Learning from Pictures: A Review and Bibliography*. Bloomington, Indiana: School of Education, Indiana University. 1973. 94p.

Summary and bibliography of psychological research on how children and adults learn from pictures. Focuses on cognitive response to pictures with some discussion of affective response. For those who wish to explore the empirical underpinnings of visual design.

Lieberman, J. Ben. *Type and Typefaces*. 2nd edition. New Rochelle, New York: Myriade Press. 1977. 142p.

An introduction to typography, written in a popular style. Intended to educate the reader in the range and variety of typefaces, not to serve as a manual or technical sourcebook. Emphasis on the history of type and milestones in its invention and development. Appendix has 20 pages of typeface examples.

Linker, Jerry Mac. *Designing Instructional Visuals: Theory, Composition, Implementation*. Austin, Texas: Instructional Media Center, University of Texas. 1968. 35p.

A small book about the fundamentals of design, written for teachers. Presents basic requirements for producing effective instructional visuals. Discusses communication strategies and reasons for using visuals. Simply written at an introductory level with appropriate line illustrations.

Macaulay, David. *The Way Things Work*. Boston: Houghton Mifflin. 1988. 384p.

An ambitious compendium of visual explanations for how commonplace machines operate, with entries ranging from can openers and pianos to supermarket check-out systems. Each is illustrated through effective line drawings, often magnified and colored for clarification. Shows how visual images can effectively communicate concepts and complex processes. A glossary of technical terms and an index are included.

MacGregor, A.J. *Graphics Simplified: How to Plan and Prepare Effective Charts, Graphs, Illustrations, and Other Visual Aids*. Toronto: University of Toronto Press. 1979. 64p.

Legibility is the key word in this short guide to preparing instructional graphics. Shows how graphics can be made legible by choosing appropriate illustrations, adapting information to a specific medium, and preparing charts and graphics carefully. A practical book of tips and suggestions.

March, Marion. *Creative Typography*. Cincinnati: North Light Books. 1988. 144p.

An approachable and friendly book on typography. Covers the basic ground of type fonts, sizes, spacing, color, and arrangement while engendering a playful and inventive attitude toward type use. Examples are plentiful and particularly well suited to the text. The second half of the book consists of projects and exercises to stimulate imaginative solutions to practical typographical problems.

McKim, Robert H. *Experiences in Visual Thinking*. Monterey, California: Brooks/Cole Publishing. 1972. 171p.

An invitation to engage in visual thinking. Takes a psychological/perceptual approach toward improving visualization skills. Step-by-step guidance to bring the reader through three stages: (1) awareness of thinking; (2) heightened observation; (3) sketching ideas. Relaxed tone, with many exercises, puzzles, and thinking challenges. (A slightly reworked version of this book was published in 1980 under the title *Thinking Visually*.)

Morgan, Hal. *Symbols of America*. New York: Viking. 1986. 239p.

A compilation of North American brand names and trademarks for familiar products. Entries are organized by type, e.g., animal, plant, sport, and reach back into the early part of this century. The text is more anecdotal than analytical, but provides interesting information on how trademarks evolved to market specific products.

Morgan, John and Peter Welton. *See What I Mean: An Introduction to Visual Communication*. London: Edward Arnold. 1986. 133p.

An attempt to provide the general reader with a background in current theories and models of visual communication, including discussion of pertinent research. Examples are drawn from diverse media and cultures. Useful discourse on the vocabulary of visual perception.

Murgio, Matthew P. *Communications Graphics*. New York: Van Nostrand Reinhold. 1969. 240p.

Despite its broad title, this book deals mainly with the design and production of charts for visual presentation. Discusses effective and ineffective mechanics of data display, selection of appropriate media, use of color, and facilities planning. Examples are bold and plentiful.

Murphy, John and Michael Rowe. *How to Design Trademarks and Logos*. Cincinnati: North Light Books. 1988. 144p.

Presents trademark and logo design through hypothetical and actual case studies. Discusses issues of design and conceptualization, ideal editing, product placement, and legalities of the marketplace. Bright, slick examples from advertising bombard the reader with graphic alternatives. Gives insight into the consideration of several design possibilities for a single product.

Nelson, Roy Paul. *The Design of Advertising*. 4th Edition. Dubuque, Iowa: William C. Brown. 1981. 383p.

A handbook of advertising design for all types of media: television, magazines, newspapers, radio, and direct mail. Gives down-to-earth advice on ad design, with practical, detailed explanations of design elements and many illustrations of ads that work. Shows the creative side of advertising against a backdrop of commonly encountered constraints. Includes assignments for practice.

Nelson, Roy Paul. *Publication Design*. Dubuque, Iowa: William C. Brown. 1972. 232p.

A manual for art directors, editors, and journalists, written with an understanding of the work relationships among these professions. Major emphasis on magazine production, including format, typography, use of art, cover and page design, and the production process. Gives brief history of magazine production.

Newcomb, John. *The Book of Graphic Problem-Solving*. New York: Bowker. 1984. 259p.

A word-oriented approach to graphic art design. Describes the "bite system" whereby graphic ideas are generated by analyzing key words in the message. Gives lists of questions for brainstorming and traces the thinking process from early sketches through finished design. Presents twelve basic tools for creating visual surprise. Full-color examples are covers and advertising from contemporary magazines.

Novitz, David. *Pictures and Their Use in Communication: A Philosophical Essay*. The Hague: Martinus Nijhoff. 1977. 165p.

Philosophical treatise on the ways in which pictures are used to inform and influence our thinking, attitudes, and perceptions of the world. The first part of the book considers the practice of pictorial representation and the growth of pictorial style. The second part explores the use of pictures to communicate and the logic in choosing picture types. Chapter Six considers the cognitive and emotional effects of pictures on the viewer.

Pedersen, B. Martin. *Graphis Diagram 1*. Zurich: The Graphis Press. 1988. 282p.

One of the great inspirational books in the visual communication library. Full color, full illustration, and full of ideas. Required "reading" for all graphic designers. Examples are from around the world and cover such topics as: History, statistical diagrams, flow diagrams, technical diagrams, maps, plans and scientific diagrams.

Pettersson, Rune. *Visuals for Information: Research and Practice*. Englewood Cliffs, New Jersey: Educational Technology Publications. 1989. 315p.

A broad-based text on visual communication, drawn across the fields of perception, language, information science, and graphic design. Explores relationship between verbal and visual communication. Chapter 4 nicely integrates research findings into the practical aspects of design. Text is very readable; illustrations are sparse.

Pilditch, James. *Communication by Design*. London: McGraw-Hill. 1970. 194p.

A study of corporate identity through graphic design. Discusses visual communication and how industry, art, technology, and communication interrelate in this field. Written from the perspective of management and marketing to explore how a visual image helps to establish an identity throughout all levels of corporate operations. Well illustrated.

Porter, Tom and Sue Goodman. *Manual of Graphic Techniques 3*. New York: Charles Scribner's Sons. 1983. 128p.

This third book in a series considers wider design techniques with an emphasis on lettering, model-making, reproductive processes, and print making. Like its predecessors, the book is organized into step-by-step processes effectively illustrated with line drawings. These books are action-oriented, offering experiences in both basic and innovative techniques.

Porter, Tom and Bob Greenstreet. *Manual of Graphic Techniques 1*. New York: Charles Scribner's Sons. 1980. 128p.

Designed as a support handbook for designers. Each page consists of line drawings and text that teach a specific design process or technique. Some are traditional, others inventive. Techniques cover surface, line, and tone; use of color; orthographic and perspective drawing; reproductive and simulation techniques; and presentation and exhibition. For the hands-on designer.

Richardson, Graham T. *Illustrations*. Clifton, New Jersey: Humana Press. 1985. 337p.

An ambitious, educational guide to all types and varieties of illustrations. The introduction briefly runs through the principles of design. The remainder of the book explains kinds and uses of illustration, with much attention devoted to equipment and materials used in production and duplication. Some black-and-white illustration.

Robertson, Bruce. *How to Draw Charts and Diagrams*. Cincinnati: North Light Books. 1988. 192p.

A step-by-step handbook for understanding, selecting, and accurately constructing charts. Each page is a well-illustrated lesson on a specific consideration in chart design or production. Differentiates among charts that show relationships; length, area, and volume; graphs; maps. Includes scales and formulas to ensure accurate proportions and an appendix of basic grids to use for plotting charts. Examples of effective and ineffective charts.

Romano, Frank J. *The TypEncyclopedia*. New York: Bowker. 1984. 188p.

An alphabetical presentation of over 100 main terms in the field of typography, attractively and thoroughly illustrated. Terms reflect typology as accepted practice, as applied art, and as technological function. Helpful for solving problems or to read through as a primer.

Rosen, Ben. *The Corporate Search for Visual Identity: A Study of Fifteen Outstanding Corporate Design Programs*. New York: Van Nostrand Reinhold. 1970. 259p.

An analysis of 15 corporate visual symbols. Explains rationale for pursuing a visual identity, the task of the graphic designer, and the process of developing an image. Attests to the powerful influence of graphic symbols on product identification and corporate success. Generously illustrated with photographs and graphic art.

Scott, Robert Gillam. *Design Fundamentals.* New York: McGraw-Hill. 1951. 199p.

An older book lacking the dramatic illustration of more recent publications on this subject, but offering a clear and thoughtful presentation of basic design elements. Perhaps its most useful feature is its final section, in which these elements are applied in a walk-through of the book's own design and production.

Shulevitz, Uri. *Writing with Pictures.* New York: Watson-Guptill. 1985. 271p.

Intended as a guide for illustrators of children's books, this book presents elements of design in a simple, introductory style. Includes a thorough discussion of sequencing, storyboarding, use of space and composition, and drawing simple figures, with illustrative examples from children's literature.

A Sign Systems Manual. New York: Praeger Publishers. 1970. 76p.

A grammar for sign designers. Illustrates a basic system for designing, constructing, and displaying signs. Gives a survey and history of alphabets and typography. Presents conventions governing use of lettering, symbol, type, color, and spacing. Examples of professionally designed signs.

Skal, David. *Graphic Communications for the Performing Arts.* New York: Theatre Communications Group. 1981. 152p.

A small reference library of graphic images used to promote the performing arts. The book focuses on the arts in America but provides several examples from abroad for comparison. A fascinating look at how a field devoted to aesthetics has adapted graphic design to its purposes.

Smith, Laura J. *The Development of a Symbol.* New York: Wittenborn and Company. 1966. Unpaged.

The story of a single design task from start to finish. A record of the thought processes and variations in design during the development of the Peace Corps symbol. Discussion emphasizes the evolution of meaning in the design rather than the technical processes of production.

Smith, Robert Charles. *Basic Graphic Design.* Englewood Cliffs, New Jersey: Prentice-Hall. 1986. 164p.

Although intended for beginners, this book assumes some familiarity with the vocabulary and process of design. Illustrations tend toward the sophisticated, but are varied in kind and style. Includes in-depth treatment of format and layout.

Souter, Nick and Stuart Newman. *Creative Director's Sourcebook.* London: Quarto Publishing. 1988. 318p.

An oversized volume that brings together samples of visual advertising from 1850 through the 1980's. The examples, all beautifully reproduced in full color, are drawn from several countries and arranged by decade. Subject matter is diverse, from endorsements for soaps and cars to political posters from the Russian revolution. Intended as a stimulus for a dry brain, this book would also be useful in recreating design from a given era.

Squibb, Sharon. *Studio Techniques for Advertising Agencies and Graphic Designers*. New York: Watson-Guptill. 1991. 144p.

A handbook of basic studio techniques that apply to both the drawing board and the computer. Describes and illustrates the fine variation in design that can be achieved through careful use of type, photographs, and photocopies. Covers the basics, with handy chapters on tricks of the trade and computer graphics.

Stankowski, Anton. *Visual Presentation of Invisible Processes*. Tuefen, Switzerland: Arthur Niggi Ltd. 1968. 127p.

Graphic images ranging form advertising to fine art, grouped by theme or technique, with brief commentary. Selections span the 20th century, with many dating back to the emergence of graphic art in the 1920s. Stankowski's purpose is to show design as an illustration of process rather than as the depiction of an object. Made for browsing with no table of contents or index.

Stevens, Peter S. *Handbook of Regular Patterns: An Introduction to Symmetry in Two Dimensions*. Cambridge; Massachusetts: MIT Press. 1980. 400p.

A compendium of repeating designs, organized according to established notions of symmetry and symmetry operations. Presents wealth of patterns, with special attention to the work of M.C. Escher. The large collection of border patterns is particularly noteworthy. Stimulates independent pattern-making by conveying the idea that some design units will generate repeating patterns. Includes exercises for analysis, but not production, of designs.

Swann, Alan. *How to Understand and Use Design and Layout*. Cincinnati: North Light Books. 1987. 144p.

A well-illustrated primer to help develop a sense of design composition and the page as a field of space. Examples are plentiful and aptly captioned to heighten the reader's visual sense and judgment. For each example, applications of line, position, type, and color are gradually accumulated to achieve effective design. A good starting point for beginners.

Thiel, Philip. *Visual Awareness and Design*. Seattle: University of Washington Press. 1981. 287p.

A textbook to teach design to students of environmental planning, design, and management. Instruction based on a comparison of visual with structural design. A step-by-step approach that builds from simple appreciation to technical execution. Presents integrated sequences of problems, exercises, readings, and quizzes. Thorough explanations of the vocabulary of design. Text is supplemented by thought-provoking quotes from noted people in the field of visual perception.

Thompson, Bradbury. *Bradbury Thompson: The Art of Graphic Design*. New Haven: Yale University Press. 1988. 218p.

A retrospective of graphic design from the career of designer Bradbury Thompson. It is like a "time lapse camera" portrait of the development of avant garde graphic art through the middle of this century. Shows experimentation with typeface, alphabets, and inks as well as trends in magazine covers and postage stamps. Large pages with bold, slick illustrations.

Thompson, Philip and Peter Davenport. *Dictionary of Graphic Language.* New York: St. Martin's Press. 1980. 258p.

An international alphabetical listing of graphic images used in advertising. Brief meaning given for most images, which include religious, artistic, erotic, and psychological symbols. Shows a certain fondness for the dramatic and bizarre. Also published under the title *The Dictionary of Graphic Images.*

Tufte, Edward R. *Envisioning Information.* Cheshire, Connecticut: Graphics Press. 1990. 126p.

Addresses the question of how to display complex, dynamic information (e.g., dance movements, Euclidian geometry, aerial maps) on the flatland of print on paper (or video screen). Drawing examples from Galileo to Lichtenstein, Tufte analyzes how large amounts of complex data can be layered, separated, colored and encoded. The accompanying analysis is well wrought and insightful.

Tufte, Edward R. *The Visual Display of Quantitative Information.* Cheshire, Connecticut: Graphics Press. 1983. 197p.

An in-depth discussion of the principles that underlie effective graphic display. Uses examples to identify excellence and mediocrity in the design of graphs. Gives guidelines for use of data-ink, suggestions for the avoidance of irrelevant and obfuscating lines, and instruction on how to edit graphs. Includes formulas for evaluating the cleanness and integrity of graphic displays.

Van Dyke, Scott. *From Line to Design: Design Graphics Communication.* West Lafayette, Indiana: PDA Publishers. 1982. 160p.

Intended as a supplemental text for students of environmental design. Presents a series of exercises on design considerations for visual communication. Instruction moves from representation of abstract concepts to technical rendering of architectural detail. Detailed treatment of principles of simplicity, organization, style, and attention-directing devices. Uses interesting combinations of photographs and illustrations.

White, Jan V. *Using Charts and Graphs: 1000 Ideas for Visual Persuasion.* New York: Bowker. 1984. 202p.

An indispensable book for visualizing data using charts and graphs. Emphasizes that understanding the content of a chart is crucial to its appropriate visualization. Bountifully illustrated, with a playful attitude that encourages experimentation and creativity. All kinds of diagrams are considered. Discussion encompasses basic design considerations as well as specific suggestions for chart and graph design. Stimulating to browse.

White, Jan V. *Mastering Graphics: Design and Production Made Easy.* New York: Bowker. 1983. 180p.

A common-sense introduction to using graphics. Begins with a discussion about relating design to purpose and the role of decision-making in the design process. Breezy style, but rooted in solid advice about using logos, typography, photographs, pictures, and color. Also offers practical information on paper selection, printing, and finishing. Amply illustrated.

White, Jan V. *Designing for Magazines: Common Problems, Realistic Solutions.* 2nd edition. New York: Bowker. 1982. 210p.

A companion volume to *Editing by Design* that applies design concepts and techniques to typical problems in magazine production. Offers sound advice on cover design, tables of contents, editorials and features, and the presentation of new products. Written with clarity and humor; illustrated with sketches and photos of published materials.

White, Jan V. *Editing by Design: A Guide to Effective Word-and-Picture Communication for Editors and Designers.* 2nd edition. New York: Bowker. 1982. 248p.

An introduction to design that incorporates visual thinking into the presentation of basic concepts and techniques of creating publications. Written from the vantage point of magazine production, with special attention to page design, use of type and color, and various ways to use illustrative materials effectively. Lots of examples, lists of common pitfalls, and good practical advice.

White, Jan V. *The Graphic Idea Notebook.* Revised edition. Rockport, Massachusetts: Rockport Publishers. 1991. 206p.

Seeks to debunk concept of graphic art as esoteric and replace it with common sense. Ready reference manual to be used as "sparkplug for ideas." Organized around problems commonly faced; offers alternative solutions that are feasible. Illustrations are large and engaging. Handy for troubleshooting or to leaf through for inspiration.

White, Tony. *The Animator's Workbook.* New York: Watson-Guptill. 1986. 160p.

An introduction to the basic principles of animation, with bold, colorful illustrations throughout. Useful for its straightforward explanations of simple drawing techniques and its sketches of figures in various stages of motion.

Wildbur, Peter. *Information Graphics: A Survey of Typographic, Diagrammatic, and Cartographic Communication.* New York: Van Nostrand Reinhold. 1989. 144p.

Wibur uses a case study approach to communicating information in graphic form. The focus is on technical information. Some history. Very well illustrated.

Wildbur, Peter. *International Trademark Design.* New York: Van Nostrand Reinhold. 1979. 135p.

Primarily a collection of trademarks, with a brief discussion of trademark history and the practical aspects of trademark design. A resource to browse for ideas.

Wileman, Ralph E. *Exercises in Visual Thinking.* New York: Hastings House. 1980. 124p.

Posits that the skill of thinking visually underlies the development and appropriate use of instructional materials. Practical guidance for visualizing facts, directions, processes, data, and concepts. Nurtures a widened perception that recognizes gradations between the concrete and the abstract and that appreciates clarity, unity, and imagination in visual design. Discussion of the relationship between visual and verbal elements. Sequential exercises provided.

Willows, D.M. and H.A. Houghton, eds. *Basic Research*. New York: Springer-Verlag. 1987. 214p. Vol. 1 of The Psychology of Illustration.

A serious effort to bring together results of research from the many disciplines that investigate visual perception. Considers the psychological and instructional issues that surround illustrated learning materials. This volume focuses on theoretical and empirical research issues, including the effects of pictures on memory and processing, and how viewers perceive graphs, diagrams, charts, and other illustrated educational materials. Includes an extensive bibliography. See also: Houghton, H.A. and D.M. Willows, eds. *Instructional Issues*. Vol. 2 of The Psychology of Illustration.

Winters, Arthur and Shirley F. Milton. *The Creative Connection: Advertising Copyrighting and Idea Visualization*. New York: Fairchild Publications. 1982. 193p.

The second half of this book is a pertinent discussion of idea visualization as it applies to effective advertising. Chapters 9, 10, and 11 suggest how to brainstorm visual expressions and present basic techniques for cartooning ideas. Tips on simple sketching may prove most useful for developing storyboards.

Wright, Andrew. *Designing for Visual Aids*. New York: Van Nostrand Reinhold. 1970. 96p.

Links the need for visual aids to the evolution in teaching and learning methods. Begins with an introduction to design principles and audience analysis. Gives brief overview of each media type, its characteristics and teaching use, and observations on its design and production. The third section deals with the design of educational material with attention to clarity, recognition, expression, figure/ground relationships, use of space, color, and line.

Zelazny, Gene. *Say It with Charts: The Executive's Guide to Successful Presentations*. Homewood, Illinois: Dow Jones-Irwin. 1985. 130p.

Practical advice on choosing and using charts for the display of data. Emphasis on analyzing data to determine the relationship to be visualized. Provides problems in data display with solutions. Includes a portfolio of 80 charts that vary by purpose and complexity.

Zimmer, Ann and Fred Zimmer. *Visual Literacy in Communication: Designing for Development*. Bucks, England: Hulton Educational Publications. 1978. 144p.

Tackles practical concerns in designing culture-sensitive visual materials to foster literacy. Offers realistic guidelines useful to all designers of visual materials. Includes checklists and specifications forms for producing and analyzing visual images.

A

Animation, 85
Appropriateness of visuals, 82
Arbitrary graphics, 13
   (See also) Graphic symbols
Area graphs, 38
Attitudes, visualizing, 62
Audience
   aiding memory of, 97
   characteristics of, affecting
      choice of kind and degree of
      visualization, 29
   connecting with existing
      knowledge held by, 94
   directing attention of, 82-83
   focusing on center of attention,
      92
   gaining attention of, 96
   holding interest of, 97

B

Bar graphs, 41-42
Boldness of words and images, 80-81

C

Chronologies, visualizing, 58-59
Circle graphs, 39-40
   hint for using, 39
Clarity, 79-87
   appropriateness relevant to, 82
   boldness important to, 80-81
   contrast affecting, 81
   eliminating nonessential
      information to improve, 83-84
   establishing shots and zooming to
      improve, 85
   panning or tilting to increase,
      85
   progressive disclosure enhancing,
      84
   rating sheet for, 120
   relationship between readability
      and size, 79-80
   simple animation enhancing, 86
   visual devices to aid, 82-83
Concept-related graphics, 13
   (See also) Graphic symbols
Concepts
   invisible, 59-62
   visible, 54-59
   visualizing, 54-62
Content analysis, affecting choice
   of kind and degree of
   visualization, 29
Contrast, contributing to clarity,
   81

D

Dale, Edgar, 7
Degrees of visualization, 18-24
   and audience characteristics , 29
   and content analysis, 29
   emphasized pictorial or graphic
      symbol frame type, 25
   emphasized reader frame type,
      20-21
   factors affecting choice of,
      29-30
   and instructional objectives, 29
   and medium of instruction, 29
   pictorial or graphic symbol frame
      type, 26
   pictorial or graphic symbol frame
      with verbal cues to meaning
      type, 24
   reader frame type, 20
   reader frame with no visual cues
      to meaning type, 22
   and time and resource
      availability, 29-30
   using, 27
   verbal/visual balanced frame
      type, 23
   and visual thinking ability, 30
Dewey, John, 7
Diethelm, Walter J., 14
Directions, visualizing, 50-52
Dreyfus, Henry, 14

E

Emphasis in visuals, 20-21, 25
Essential information, limiting
   visuals to, 83-84
Establishing shot, 85

F

Facts, visualizing, 49
Feelings or attitudes, visualizing,
   62
Field testing visuals, 105-106
Form and Communication, 14

G

Generalizations, visualizing, 59-60
Graphic design, importance of, 79
Graphic symbols, 11, 13, 14-16
   arbitrary, 13
   concept-related, 13
   evaluating, 14
   image-related, 13
   sources of inspiration for design
      of, 14

Graphis Annual, 14
Graphs, 38-46
  area graphs, 38
  bar graphs, 41-42
  checking choices, 16
  circle graphs, 39-40
  line graphs, 40-41
  map/area graphs, 44-45
  pictorial graphs, 43-44
  titling of, 46
  types of, 39-45

I

Image-related graphics, 13
  (See also) Graphic symbols
Imagination, 94-97
  assisting viewer's memory, 97
  connecting visuals to learner's
    existing knowledge, 94
  and consistency of visual style,
    95
  getting viewer's attention, 96
  holding viewer's interest, 97
  rating sheet for, 122
Instructional objectives, affecting
    choice of kind and degree of
    visualization, 29
Instructions, aided by
    visualizations, 52
Invisible concepts
  feelings or attitudes, 62
  generalizations, 59-60
  hint for creating visualizations
    of, 62
  theories, 61
  visualizing, 59-62

L

Layout, 88-90
  importance of, 90
  tools for, 89
Line graphs, 40-41

M

Map/area graphs, 44-45
Maps, 56-57
Margins, 90
Medium of instruction, affecting
    choice of kind and degree of
    visualization, 29

N

Numerical data
  graphs used to present, 38-46
  hint for using photographs with,
    44
  tables used to present, 38
  visualizing, 38-48

O

Organizational charts, 55-60

P

Panning, 85
Photographs, hint for using, 44
Pictorial graphs, 43-44
Pictorial symbols, 11, 13
Plans, 54-55
Processes, visualizing, 53
Progressive disclosure, 84

R

Readability, 79-81
Rendering visuals, 26, 106-107

S

Screen, filling, 91
Script writing, 27
Sequencing techniques, 84
Size of words and images, 79-80
Storyboard forms, 115-119
Storyboards, 27
Symbols. *(See)* Graphic symbols
Symbol Sourcebook, 14

T

Theories, visualizing, 61
Tilting, 85
Time and resource availability,
    affecting choice of kind and
    degree of visualization,
    29-30

U

Unity, 88-93
  focusing viewers on center of
    attention, 92
  full screen improving, 91
  layout important to, 88-90
  linking words and pictures, 92
  margin affecting, 90
  rating sheet for, 121
  and visual supporting subject
    matter, 92

V

Verbal labels, importance of
    placement of, 92
Verbal presentations, compared with
    visual presentations, 3-5
Verbal symbols, 13
Verbalization
  compared with visualization, 5-6
  value of, linked to reading, 5

Visible concepts
  chronologies, 58-59
  maps, 56-57
  plans and organizational charts,
    54-55
  visualizing, 54-59
Visual design considerations, 79-97
  clarity, 79-87
  clarity rating sheet, 120
  imagination, 94-97
  imagination rating sheet, 122
  revised visuals, 100-102
  unity, 88-93
  unity rating sheet, 121
Visual devices, to direct viewer
    attention, 82-83
Visual presentations
  compared with verbal
    presentations, 3-5
  improving, 5
  uses of, 3, 5
Visualization
  (See also) Visuals
  able to represent range of
    educational messages, 6-7
  adding emphasis to, 20-21, 25
  alternative solutions to
    exercises, 32-34
  as a new language, 6-7
  as a process, 7-8
  compared with verbalization, 5-6
  conceptualization important in
    developing, 7
  degrees of, 18-26. (See also)
    Degrees of visualization
  for designing educational
    material, 7-8
  reasons for choice of, 5-6
Visuals
  (See also) Visualization
  aiding viewer's memory, 97
  audience characteristics
    affecting choice of, 29
  choice of symbols for, 13-14
  connecting with learner's
    existing knowledge, 94
  consistency of style important
    to, 95
  content analysis affecting choice
    of, 29
  design considerations for. (See)
    Visual design considerations
  directing viewer's attention,
    82-83
  emphasis in, 20-21, 25
  factors affecting choice of,
    29-30
  field testing, 105-106
  focusing viewers on center of
    attention, 92
  gaining viewer's attention, 96
  graphic symbols, 11, 13, 14-16

  hints for creating, 18, 81, 83,
    89, 91, 92, 94
  hints for reviewing, 86, 93, 97
  holding viewer's interest, 97
  instructional objectives
    affecting choice of, 29
  kinds of, 11-18
  medium of instruction affecting
    choice of, 29
  pictorial symbols, 11, 13
  placement of verbal labels in, 92
  rendering, 26, 106-107
  time and resource availability
    affecting choice of, 29-30
  using, 27
  verbal symbols, 13
  visual thinking ability affecting
    choice of, 30
Visual thinking
  alternative solutions to
    exercises, 63-77
  defined, 37
  visualizing concepts, 54-62
  visualizing facts, directions,
    and processes, 49-53
  visualizing numerical data, 38-48
Visual thinking ability, affecting
    choice of kind and degree of
    visualization, 30

Z

Zooming, 85